Four Book Endorsements for *Trusted Knowledge for Parents*

"This book, *Trusted Knowledge for Parents*, is a must read for parents with children of any age still looking for ways to improve their parenting skills. It provides positive and practical approaches to sound parenting advice sprinkled with wisdom.

Dr. Culp has written this book in a parent-friendly form and at all levels of parenting skills. She has included many topics of concern with suggestions and ideas on how to address them at home, at school and in the community.

It is a keeper! After you have read the entire book, you will want to keep it close at hand as a quick reference. It is the ideal book to share with friends, neighbors and co-worker who you want to see become better parents. Parents will surely feel the support of the author throughout this book."

Merian T. Ezzard
former middle school counselor

"As an educator, with forty plus years of experience as a classroom teacher and principal, I have read many books on parenting. Dr. Culp's book stands alone, it is a practical, enlightening book that will be a source of inspiration and guidance for parents who are impacted by the many challenges of our global society. I highly recommend it, not only for parents, but for anyone who works closely with children. Thank you, Dr. Culp, all is not lost!"

Dr. Brenda Jones Lewis
educator/consultant, Georgia

"*Trusted Knowledge for Parents: Tips to Prepare, Position, and Empower Today's Parents* delivers thoughtful, succinct and insightful advice. A must-read for those entrusted with raising responsible, resilient and capable children in a competitive world that is rapidly changing. Dr. Culp helps us to look beyond parenting in the traditional modicum. Instead, she explains parenting in a fiduciary way that is the ultimate long term investment."

Haroldeen Swearingen, EdS
adjunct professor, Mercer University

"After reading excerpts from *Trusted Knowledge for Parents,* I am convinced that the wisdom it contains is the most valuable information I have ever read to help parents raise confident, smart, and successful children. Cheers to Dr. Barbara D. Culp for having the insight to write such a powerful and compact book. It is a must-read for all parents and would be parents!"

Annie Gist
local unit president
10th District Director for Georgia PTA

Trusted Knowledge
for Parents

Words of Wisdom

Barbara D. Culp

Glean knowledge and wisdom from the experiences of someone who has successfully traversed the roads of education. Written for educators and learners in all walks of the educational journey, *Words of Wisdom* provides a collection of guiding principles, practical advice, and encouraging words for both beginners and veterans in the world of education.

Other Titles in This Series

Trusted Knowledge for Parents

Tips to Prepare, Position, and Empower Today's Parents

Barbara D. Culp

ROWMAN & LITTLEFIELD
Lanham • Boulder • New York • London

Published by Rowman & Littlefield
A wholly owned subsidiary of The Rowman & Littlefield Publishing Group, Inc.
4501 Forbes Boulevard, Suite 200, Lanham, Maryland 20706
www.rowman.com

Unit A, Whitacre Mews, 26-34 Stannary Street, London SE11 4AB

British Library Cataloguing in Publication Information Available

Library of Congress Cataloging-in-Publication Data Available

ISBN: 978-1-4758-3312-6 (pbk. : alk. paper)
ISBN: 978-1-4758-3313-3 (electronic)

♾™ The paper used in this publication meets the minimum requirements of
American National Standard for Information Sciences—Permanence of Paper for
Printed Library Materials, ANSI/NISO Z39.48-1992.

Printed in the United States of America

This book is dedicated to all the parents across the world who, like mine, want nothing but the best for their children; so they make tremendous sacrifices every day so that their children can be all that their Maker would have them become. Their perseverance signals an unconditional love that all good parents offer to their children.

Adolph and Gladys Daughtry never had the benefit of advanced degrees; instead, they had an abiding faith in their Maker to make all things equal. They never had to go to court or jail for any of their children, and never had to rely on government assistance for their existence. Through hard work, strong family values, and an abiding faith in our Maker, we survived and grew. They used trusted knowledge as a guiding light to raise their children. As the oldest of the six, I offer that all of the Daughtry children attended college, four finished, and two of the four earned doctoral degrees.

AS I GROW UP

By Helene Rothschild

Please...

Treat me more as a friend and less as a child. That helps me feel like an equal and encourages me to act more mature.

Problem-solve with me appropriate boundaries and guidelines. That will help me know you care and keep my agreements.

Understand that I may need to spend a lot of time with my friends. I learn important social skills with my peers.

Be guided by my level of maturity. Then you can clearly see who I am and make the appropriate decisions.

Realize that times have changed. Then you'll base your opinions on the present and not the past.

Forgive me when I make mistakes. That will help me learn how to forgive myself and others.

Teach me how to be responsible with money. Then I can learn how to be financially independent.

Accept that my values may be different than yours. That will help me feel okay and respect our differences.

Encourage me to keep my room safe but allow me my private space. Then I can learn how to honor your space and privacy.

Remember that I always need your love and support. That helps me love myself, feel secure and make the right decisions.

Thank you for preparing me for life. I love you!

Contents

Foreword

As I began to write the foreword to Dr. Barbara D. Culp's incredible book, *Trusted Knowledge for Parents*, I received a phone call from one of the homicide detectives with the Atlanta Police Department. "We need your help. A child has been murdered and we need someone here for the family," he stated. I grabbed my purse and my umbrella and ran out the door.

With the rain fiercely coming down, I arrived at the crime scene. I looked around noticing the blank faces of strangers and neighbors who were in awe of this child lying dead in the middle of the street. The mother screamed—the scream that I had heard many times before. A scream that comes from the depths of your soul that is indescribable yet never forgotten.

The following questions arise in my mind, "What could the parents of this child have done to prevent this from happening? Could there have been different choices made? Even in his young life, was it a life fulfilled and sustained by parental encouragement?" There were a lot of things that ran in and out of my mind. Ironically, at that moment, it dawned on me that there was a reason for me writing the foreword to this book. It was not just to give the regular insightful view of "this is a great resource" or "I highly recommend this book." No, there is a purpose for all things, especially when doing things that can bring about a wonderful outcome. This is one of those times.

I read the book and was going to give a different perspective based simply off of the writing of the book, but it deserves so much more.

Being a mother of a murdered child and a thirty-year victims' advocate, I know firsthand about losing a child and how we as parents tend to assume the responsibility of such a tragedy. We question the choices we've made. "Did I influence my child as best as possible to be a responsible person of our society? Did I tell them that they were special . . . that they were loved . . . that they could become anybody that they wanted to become?"

Our choices in life whether we choose to be influenced or be the influencer, the follower or perhaps the leader, these are questions that we ask ourselves as parents. To know better is to do better, and this book offers a vivid insight into steps of making better choices. *Trusted Knowledge for Parents* is just that, words of knowledge. It offers the canniness of one educator that humbly and honestly shares her wisdom as an educator but more so in the prospective of knowing the growing pains of raising children in general. She has taken the experiences of a lifetime and have mixed them into an auspicious tall glass of knowledge. This blended wealth of practicality is not just suited for one particular type of parent but applicable to all parents.

The impeccable wisdom that is shared in this book is a must-read for maintaining sustainable growth between a parent and a child. Far too often we look at others and point the finger at the problems that exist in our world. This book gives a keen direction of your duties as a parent to direct and guide your child into being the best person that they can possibly become.

Dr. Culp is a parent in every aspect of the word. She is unapologetic in admitting that she made numerous mistakes with her own kids and failed at various attempts to be the "best" parent. She helps the reader understand that being a parent doesn't come with directions so honestly, how would we know if what we're doing as parents is right or wrong?

This book serves as that guide like a compass, to the unforeseen world of parenting. Most importantly, this book shows the importance of what is being read by breaking each part down in the most simplistic way that parents of all backgrounds are able to comprehend. The different passages reverently influence the life of a child in so many facets. She divides the book into three categories, showing an emphasis on "Trusted Knowledge for Your Child," "Trusted Knowledge for You," and "Trusted Knowledge for Your Outlook." Centering on these categories, she then begins to define, show the benefit, and explain how to apply ways to utilize this knowledge in different aspects of your life.

This book is part of a series of books that is encouraging, suggestive, relatable, and mostly informative. It stands true to its title, *Trusted Knowledge for Parents*, as it inspires the reader to know that in a place of wisdom there is always clarity that our choices are what defines us and defines our children. As Dr. Culp states, "Children mimic the elements in their environment." Remembering back on that rainy afternoon in Atlanta, it makes me think of all the important topics that this book touches on and I can't help but to think of that parent that no longer has the opportunity to raise her son. I think of myself and my deceased son and knowing the mistakes I made and wish I had the opportunity to do it all over again. I would have certainly utilized this book as a helpful guide to parenting.

As a gesture of "Pay It Forward" and community service, I am inviting all parents to read this book. It will assist with developing the positive parenting skills needed to groom our generation of productive citizens. Throughout the book, a great deal of emphasis is placed on the relationship with teachers and administrators as these are some of the people who oftentimes spend more time with your children than you do. This book is a must-read for parents worldwide!

Happy parenting,

Brenda J. Muhammad
Founder/President—Mothers of Murdered Sons/Daughters (MOMS)
Executive Director—Atlanta Victim Assistance, Inc.
Past President—Atlanta Board of Education

Preface

The day your child came into this world, you started down a path that would define the rest of your life. If you adopted a child, have taken up caring for a relative's son or daughter, or have created that beautiful life yourself, you are first and foremost a parent. No matter where you go or what you do in life, know that you are a valuable human being. Own that personal power, because the contributions you will make to this world will shine!

Every day, you will grow and mature. Every day, you will discover new and amazing things about your strengths, your personality, and your innermost self. All the steps that you take to learn, to grow, and to become more than what you are right now will build an ever brighter future for you, your children, and your neighborhood. Everything you do for yourself will enhance the lives of the people you love!

At times, the path you have chosen will be hard. Remember that your friends, your family, and your community want you to succeed. They want to help you get closer to your dreams because you'll be a better person and will contribute more to society. Best of all, you'll be a happy person living the perfect life for you!

Remember, too, that your kids love you and want you to be happy. They want to come home to parents who are satisfied with their own place in life, and who take pride in their adult accomplishments. They want you to share the moments of your life with them as they occur. In fact, they need to see you as dynamic, growing individuals so that they can become lifelong learners!

Always model the behaviors you want and use more direct methods to ensure that your children learn to love learning. Offer to help with their homework, and stand back when they want to do it alone. Check in with your school principal or assistant principal at the beginning of the year so you know what kinds of changes to expect for your child. Engage early and often with the teachers, coaches, and counselors your kids encounter every school day. They spend almost as much time with your child as you do, so their input can be invaluable.

And don't stop there. Ask the teachers if they are planning activities that need to be chaperoned so you can plan ahead. If you can't take time off work, offer to help in other ways. Perhaps you have a special skill that can lighten the teacher's load. Be creative! Think outside the usual parent-teacher box and find new ways to engage, interact, and be supportive of their efforts.

Know, too, that learning extends to your family's history. Your past also belongs to your children. Give them that gift by telling them what life was like when you were their age, at every age! Compare what you had that they lack with what they have that you lacked. Your stories will ground them in a real and living time period. Those stories will also show how they are even now storing up their own stories to share with their children.

Whether you've parented a child into young adulthood, have just welcomed a baby into your house, or are considering how to prepare for life as a parent, you've already taken a lot of steps into your best future. Opening this book is one of them. The wisdom on these pages will help you prepare. Return to this book whenever you need to refresh your thoughts, tune your habits, or reconnect with your power. Live always as if your destiny is within reach, and you will succeed!

Acknowledgments

I acknowledge that the role of a parent is the most awesome, crucial, and difficult job on this earth. In my opinion, in fact, there is none greater! Parenting requires a lifelong commitment of unconditional love. To be chosen to shape, mold, and nurture a child's life into who his Creator wants him to become is a most worthy assignment, one that I truly believe you will be held accountable for some day.

You are to perform this job humbly, prayerfully, and reverently. You are to stay in constant communication with the Giver of this amazing gift to ensure that you are following the innate instructions, directions, and desires set forth for your replacement on earth.

So much in life depends on you getting this assignment correct. You cannot afford to get this wrong! Being a parent is a full-time job. If you can't commit to that, you would do well not to become a parent. It is not a sometime job, a part-time job, or a job you take on only when you feel like it or only when things look good. A child depends on you for everything 24/7/365. Love him, teach him, and provide everything they need to succeed and sustain themselves during their time on this planet. Awesome task, isn't it?

Today we see so many broken children, teens, and adults because their parents, who had the responsibility of nurturing them, failed along the way. Trust me because I have firsthand knowledge of this. I failed miserably with the children given to me. I wrote this book hoping to help others to get it right, to prevent them from wasting valuable time fretting over their mistakes.

Often when I watch television, drive near bridges, stroll through a park, or attend family functions, I see too many human beings living meaningless lives. From my heart, I can't help but believe that those people would not be where they are if their parents had provided more: more time, more exposures, more love, and more Christian experiences. We forget that having the biggest house, driving the most expensive car, or having the best job is not how our children become successful human beings. These things don't equate to a purpose-driven life.

Provide your children with a moral and righteous lifestyle. Start when they are in the womb. Eat right, read to them, sing to them, and pray over them. After they arrive, nurture their body and hearts. Provide for them, guard their minds, and offer a spiritual life. Children who grow up feeling unloved and not feeling good about themselves often intentionally lash out when they are grown. They hurt others and themselves because their spirits were severely wounded by so many missed opportunities. They never received the love, training, education, guidance, or gratification they so desperately needed.

As parents, we stumble. We admit our mistakes, and the lessons learned help us teach our children that we might not be perfect, but we all grow and become better. Always make your child your first priority. When they become parents, your teachings will become their own *Trusted Knowledge*!

Introduction

I have a confession to make. As a parent, I feel like I blew it!

Many times I thought that my husband and I should never have been allowed to raise one child, let alone two. We failed at every step along the way. We failed to know what to do whenever a crisis arose. We failed to give our kids a strong sense of values that would carry them through life. We failed at the little things—and boy, did we fail at the big things!

It wasn't that we didn't try, though. Far from it. Actually, I think that we tried too hard.

In hindsight, I see so many things that we could have done better. But how were we to know what was right or wrong? We had no crystal ball to show us how our decisions would impact our kids in the future. Neither of our children came with an owner's manual tailored to their personality needs, and goals and desires. We were just two people trying not to mess things up too badly.

Now, from a place of wisdom where I can clearly see all the missteps and the steps that we should have taken, I wrote this book. In these pages, you'll find three broad areas of wisdom. First comes "Trusted Knowledge for Your Child." These are my very direct and specific ideas about raising children. Many include discussions of home life and school life, so they are appropriate for any age group.

Then comes "Trusted Knowledge for You." These are ideas and directives that apply to you as a parent and as a human being. After all, your own needs don't disappear just because a child enters your life.

The third and final section is "Trusted Knowledge for Your Outlook." This section works with the concepts and attitudes that will keep you emotionally happy, psychologically healthy, and sane!

My goal is to help you raise caring, respectful, and productive children who will be good citizens at every age. A critical part of that will be the focus you turn toward your child's school. The people who walk those halls—including everyone from the janitors to the principal, from the cafeteria cooks to teachers with a lifetime of experience—are your keys to your child's future success. If you follow their guidance and trust their wisdom, they will unlock the gate so that your child will achieve a shining career and a wonderful life!

As you read through this book, you'll discover that the knowledge I offer does not judge your skills or abilities. How could I possibly judge anyone after what I failed to do as a parent? Know that these words of wisdom were forged in the crucible. They have been hardened with resolve and experience and, most importantly, with a parent's love.

A wonderful poem by Dorothy Law Nolte is called "Children Learn What They Live." Different parts of the poem point out that children mimic the elements in their environment—what they see around them is what they learn. So a hostile home filled with criticism, yelling, fighting, and abuse teaches them to be cruel, short-tempered, aggressive, and abusive. Children who are surrounded by responsibility, honesty, stability, and generosity become productive, truthful, balanced, and loving.

I invite you now to create your own poem: the poem that is your child.

Part I

Trusted Knowledge for Your Child

CREATIVE CURFEWS

Creative curfews provide your children with a clear set of rules that can be adapted for special occasions.

Creative curfews allow you to adjust rules according to your kid's maturity. Giving young kids a "bedtime curfew" helps them feel more responsible about going to bed on time. By the time they're old enough for a "coming home" curfew, they're used to the idea that this type of schedule needs to be met. Later, when the teenage years hit, the "evening curfew" will be part of an ingrained habit, which means you'll have fewer fights!

Creative curfews apply to school and homework as much as bedtime and dates! The "coming home" curfew is the time at which you expect your child to walk through the door after school every day. If you're at work, they need to text you at that time, so that you know they're safe. The "homework curfew" is the time at which they are expected to sit down to their homework. These curfews can change to accommodate after-school activities, special events, and even special projects.

Creative curfews are creative because they're adaptable. If an educational program is showing at the theater, you can lift the bedtime curfew for one night. After-school activities that happen once a week trigger a change in that day's coming home curfew, while sports events can change the evening curfew. With this system, your kids will understand that being outside the curfew isn't a pass to wild activity; it's just a change in the usual activities. They are still expected to behave!

BEFRIEND THE FRIENDS

Befriend the friends your children hang out with, so that you can guide their judgment and keep them safe.

Befriending the friends is such an important step for parents. If you don't know who your children are hanging out with, then you have no idea what kinds of habits or ideas your kids are being exposed to. You can be the best parent in the world and catch a change in their behavior or personality the moment it happens, but by then it's too late. You need to be present in their lives before those changes occur.

Befriend the friends your kids make at school. And don't pretend that you can't because you're never on the campus. Ask your child's teacher for help, and don't be shy about asking teachers who might only see your kids once a week for news. Be sure you ask for information about good friends, too—kids change as they grow, so a good friend today might not be so nice tomorrow! Nowadays, it's easier than ever to see who your kids are involved with in other ways. Monitor their social media use, check out new kids they link to, and always read their blog posts. You can't stop a freight train that is going to crash. Be there before it even leaves the station!

Befriend the friends in all areas of your kids' lives. Know your neighbors, even the teenagers and adults who might chat with your kids. Ask your children's teachers to e-mail you if they think your kids are getting involved with a rough crowd. Know where your kids hang out and the kinds of crowds that show up there. The effort can keep your kids safe, healthy, and on the right path.

HEALTHY GUIDANCE

Provide your child with *healthy guidance* about food.

Healthy guidance works best when it starts early! Babies who are fed lots of sugary foods become picky (and unhealthy) eaters, so your kids are never too young to eat well. By providing nutritious foods throughout their lives, you'll set them on a lifelong path of wellness.

Healthy guidance for school days can be tough. Your kids are probably going to be presented with a lot of unhealthy choices at school. Pack their lunches when they're young and have them pack their own lunches as they get older. Make sure they have a healthy snack for the middle of the morning when they get hungry, and they'll avoid the candy and cookies.

Healthy guidance should be part of your everyday routine. Water or milk should be the drink of choice for meals for everyone at the table, with sodas being left as special treats (and ones that are split between two people). Be aware that frozen dinners might look healthy but can be loaded with sugar or salt; cook your own meals whenever possible. Snacks like candy and cookies are fine once in a while but never give kids those oversized treats from the bakery. Instead buy a package that has smaller cookies, with five or seven being a serving, and allow everyone a half serving (two or three) of those.

CONFERENCING FOR KIDS

Conferencing for kids encourages you to attend Parent Teacher Association (PTA) conferences—and other conferences!

Conferencing for kids is about your child—and about you! Attending the PTA conference keeps you informed about the latest changes in education and at your school. Showing up shows that you care, so your child's teachers and school administrators know that they can reach out to you for anything that happens with your child's education. And your child knows that you care enough to make the extra effort!

Conferencing for kids helps your entire family. When you attend the PTA or other educational conferences, you meet other parents and professionals who are involved in your world. You get the chance to interact with others who have the same issues and hear how they solved the same problems you're facing. Best of all, you get to support others and be supported!

Conferencing for kids isn't a choice. You must connect with the individuals who control so much of your child's day. In fact, these same people are going to help your child set the course they will follow for the rest of their lives. Prime among them are school teachers. After all, they conference with your kid five times a week! Why wouldn't you want to meet them and know them? Be part of your child's educational team by showing up and getting involved face to face!

REVIEW THE REPORTS

Review the reports your school sends to track your child's progress.

Review the reports that are sent regularly by your school. The progress report will give you objective information to help you assess how your child is doing. You'll be able to pair up the numbers with the feedback from individual teachers, which affirms your trust in them. And it gives you an opening to discuss issues with your child—always an important plus!

Reviewing the reports provides you with a huge window into your child's world. You might only visit the school once in a while, and even then after school hours, so the report is a valuable source of information. One of the things to check every time is their attendance. If you notice absences that you didn't arrange, bring it up with your child right away. Don't let them think you didn't notice because they'll skip even more!

Review the reports when you are in a calm and open frame of mind. Make sure that you have settled any pressing issues that might pop up for the evening and then sit in a quiet spot. Read through the entire report to get an overview of your child's progress. Then go through a second time to revisit challenges. Think about how you can help your child resolve those challenges. Finally, go through with a highlighter and mark all the ways your child has made you proud. Then, after you've talked through the problems, you can give them plenty of praise!

GRANT PRIVACY

Grant privacy in ways that help your child grow.

Granting privacy helps your kids expand their independent natures. They learn that they can do things on their own, and that they can rely on themselves in good times and in more difficult situations. Time alone gives them the change to build their self-esteem and process their thoughts and emotions. It makes them more balanced!

Grant privacy about certain school events but not all. For example, you need to know how their schoolwork is going, but you don't need to see every assignment! Leave your intense attention for subjects where they need help or times when they ask you to step in. Create a backup system by being involved with the teachers at your school. They can always tell you if a decision you've allowed your child to make is damaging their academic efforts. By giving them the freedom to make some decisions about school on their own, your child can take charge of their own education.

Grant privacy in stages. You'll read lots of advice about age-appropriate levels of privacy, but the final judgment must be in your hands. You know your child better than anyone. What works for a daughter who is young but mature might not work for an older son who is far less mature. And every time you grant more privacy, let your kid know that it is a privilege. They can lose it if they don't use it wisely!

DOWN TIME, NOT LOUNGE TIME

Down time, not lounge time teaches your child that pleasure and relaxation don't eliminate responsibility!

Down time, not lounge time teaches a very important lesson: Just because an activity is pleasant or easy doesn't mean responsibilities are thrown out the window. You also emphasize that down time has a purpose. It allows your child the time and mental space to think things through and to figure out how to feel and the best way to act.

Down time, not lounge time enhances your child's education. Everyone needs time off from the hard work and stress they face every day, and kids are no different. When you teach them that down time can refresh their minds, they learn how to deal with bigger and bigger things. And because they know the difference between down time and being lazy, they understand important boundaries.

Give your kids *down time, not lounge time* on a regular basis. Make sure that weekends and evenings have blocks of time when your child can relax. You'll give them time to explore things that interest them beyond schoolwork and family life, which contributes to their personalities and maturity. You might also find that they will invite you into their down time, which allows you down time and quality time with your child in the same moment!

COMPETITIVE COACHING

Competitive coaching challenges kids to truly achieve their best.

Competitive coaching isn't about winning. Instead, it's about performing at the level of greatest ability and comparing that ability to others' performances. This builds the understanding that in life, they will be ranked according to their own skill and the comparative skills of others. It prepares them for the bigger world!

Competitive coaching is very important in school. Whenever your child receives a grade, be realistic about where their skill level stands. When they are just starting out with a skill, they aren't going to be able to do much, and that is perfectly acceptable! Their continued effort to meet that challenge is what counts. And they can clearly see who in the classroom puts in effort and who doesn't, so they automatically judge their own competitiveness!

Competitive coaching uses other people's performance as a measure that helps your child decide how far they want to go. Check in with teachers on what's typical for your child's age and grade level, so that you have a solid marker to use as a measuring tool. Not everyone in the world needs to understand quantum physics or Russian literature. Everyone does need to know how to balance a checkbook, set up a household budget, as well as read and write. When your children know where they stand in the group, they can decide if they should or want to advance to the next level. They choose where to put their attention so they can compete fully in their chosen field.

EAGER TO EARN

Eager to earn uses a desire or a goal to boost effort.

Eager to earn gives kids a way to practice judgment and decision-making. They learn important skills they'll need later in life; meanwhile, they're learning how to delay gratification and work toward a goal. Finally, what they do get by earning will mean more!

Eager to earn applies to school in different ways. First, to earn good grades, kids have to put in the effort. Second, to earn a spot on the sports team or a rank in the debate club, they need to work on their skills and earn their positions. Finally, to earn the trust of their teachers, they must constantly prove themselves worthy of that trust.

Make your kids *eager to earn* by starting off small. When they are very young, give them a weekly allowance they can use for toys or special activities. As they get older, transfer the cost of clothing, books, and extracurricular activities to them. And don't forget that they need to earn other things, too! They need to earn your trust, and they need to earn friendships. The only thing they don't have to earn is your love!

ENCOURAGE EFFORT

Encourage effort by offering praise every time your child honestly tries.

When you *encourage effort*, you and your child reap a lot of benefits. Your child learns that they can be as proud as trying their hand at something as they are when they succeed. Kids develop an ability to bounce back from failure when they know that effort and result are equally important. And since they learn that you value them for things other than their success, your relationship with them grows stronger.

Encourage effort at school by praising the effort that went into a work for a specific result. When your child raises their grade average or does better on a second test after receiving a lower grade on the first test, talk about the steps they took to make that happen. Work with their teacher to find out if the student's viewpoint matches the educational viewpoint. And when they line up, you can tell your child that they have considered things in a very adult manner! When you praise the individual steps, you're praising the effort they put into creating that success.

Encourage effort by asking your kids what they're going to do to achieve certain goals. If they want to save enough money to buy a toy or laptop, you can help them figure out what steps they need to take to earn enough money, and to make sure they don't spend their savings! Then praise them for each step they take. Don't praise them for efforts that are weak or too small to make a difference. That way you'll encourage real effort and build great habits.

HOUSE RULES

House rules are a set of rules that everyone must follow.

House rules provide your child (and your family) with stability and structure. They ensure that everyone does their fair share toward making the house a happy home. They teach responsibility and allow your kids to take ownership of the place where they live.

House rules apply to activities related to school. Anytime one child is working on homework or a special project, the other kids (and the adults!) are not allowed to interrupt their focus. If you have given your child a desk or table where they can work, nothing else is stored in that space, not even temporarily, by anyone else. The child has complete control and complete responsibility.

House rules range from activities to approaches. So for activities, you might have a chore list that rotates between household members every week. Activities might include a set bedtime, children packing their own lunches, or other responsibilities. Approaches cover things like obedience. Your kids might not agree with everything you say, and they are allowed to discuss why they disagree. They might actually change your mind! But in the end, they have to hold to whatever order you decide to give.

SUPPORT SPORTS

Support sports to ensure that your kids stay physically active and healthy.

Support sports because active kids are healthy physically and mentally. They get sick less and learn healthy habits. Their mental outlook becomes stronger and so they're less likely to fall into depression, anger, or behavioral issues. And sports connect them to other individuals who share the same likes!

Support sports at school by helping your child decide which activity to join. Most schools have different options, so they should be able to find something they like. Point out that teams will expect them to compete on the school's behalf. If they really want to participate just for the fun of it, steer them toward a different group outside of school.

Support sports in your home by engaging your entire family! Set up a volleyball net in the backyard. It can be used for tennis, Wiffle ball, and other games. Make walks with your kids a time of exploration in the woods or a local park. Fly a kite, play tag, or start jogging with your child. Join in, and you'll support sports in the strongest way!

GREET THE GRANDS

Greet the grands brings grandparents (and other relatives) into your child's life.

Greet the grands to give your kids the benefit of different perspectives. When relatives from different generations help your child grow, they provide a deeper sense of your family's history. Aunts and uncles can demonstrate that there are many choices in life other than the ones you selected. Many role models make for a wise child!

Greet the grands in your child's education. Whenever the relatives visit, allow them to walk the kids to school or pick them up afterward. Arrange for them to share lunch with your child or to visit during a midmorning break. If they live in the area, invite them to the volunteer opportunities and special school events. Make sure that the grandparents get to meet the child's teacher at least once. If the principal has time, take them by the office for a quick chat. Your child will recognize that their education is important to everyone, not just their parents!

Greet the grands by having them over at least once a month if they live locally. If they live farther away, see if you can arrange for a visit once in every few months. Use live video chats, e-mail, letters, and recorded videos to keep your kids in touch with their extended family. Encourage your child to share the little triumphs along with the big ones. They'll see that they are as important to their relatives as they are to you!

CHILDREN FOR CHARITY

Children for charity engages your kids in a charitable effort.

Children for charity expands your child's understanding of the world. They realize how blessed they are when they realize how much they are able to give. Rather than simply setting the example by performing charitable acts yourself, you engage your kids in the act itself. That's the best lesson of all!

Children for charity can have an astonishing impact at school. One child who takes the initiative to start a canned-food drive, a holiday gift drive, or a disaster-relief fund drive can pull together hundreds of donors! School-related charitable efforts don't have to be a huge effort to make a big impact. Something as small as sending around a collection jar or gathering bags of food on a certain day can help a lot of people.

Engage *children for charity* frequently. You might focus the spring cleaning around donations that can be given to a local goodwill. A weekly allowance can be split into a 10 percent portion for charity or a nonprofit that serves animals or the environment. Your child can round up five friends who want to help sort clothes or serve food at a local organization for a few hours. If you keep the options open, your child can pick the charities they resonate with, which builds empathy and sympathy.

FUND THE FUTURE

Fund the future by setting up a college fund early in your child's life.

Fund the future to give your child the best life possible. A college degree, or even a few years engaged in higher learning, will help them develop in an entirely different way. College teaches students how to think. Armed with minds that can focus and solve problems, your children will step into life prepared for anything.

Fund the future by tying rewards to your child's academic achievements. Whenever grades come in, provide tangible rewards for any success. It might be a grade that is at the top of the tier. Success might also be a grade that raises up from a lower level. And be sure to check in with the teacher about milestones they want your children to reach. Those can be surprising but the educational professionals know exactly how to measure success! Every milestone is worthy of celebration. Provide tangible rewards that fuel your child's investment in their own future!

Fund the future by setting up a college savings fund the day your child is born. Whenever a birthday rolls around, set aside an amount equivalent to what you've spent on the child's gifts. Every payday, drop a set amount into the fund. And be sure your child participates! Have them set aside a small percent of everything they earn for the fund. They'll grow up with the idea that they are going to college ingrained in their minds. They'll look forward to great things!

SMART SAVERS

Raise *smart savers* by opening a savings account in your child's name.

Smart savers make kids more financially aware. Even the smallest pot of money lets them know that with effort and time, they can build toward big goals and dreams. Studies show that kids who had savings accounts grow up to be adults who are much wiser about their investments. Raising smart savers is just plain smart!

Smart savers can exercise their financial common sense at school. If they want to take extracurricular activities or attend special events that cost money, they need to decide how that expense is going to be covered. They might need a uniform, special equipment, or an entry fee. Even if they don't pay for the whole thing themselves, they need to figure out where the money comes from.

Smart savers begin with a weekly allowance or some other way to earn money. Every time they receive cash for gifts or chores, they should decide how much to put away in a savings account. Notice that the choice is not whether to save—it's only how much to save! Be sure they don't put away too much of the money unless they are close to a goal. When spending is curtailed sharply for a long time, it can create a negative whiplash effect where they splurge thoughtlessly one day and lose the benefit of their long-term efforts!

HAND UPS

There are no handouts, only *hand ups.*

Teaching your kids about *hand ups* keeps them focused on the proper way to ask for and receive help. Assistance is never about having someone else do the hard work. It's always about learning something new or sharing a burden that is too large for one person. When they know the difference, they'll be able to figure out when to ask for help and when to do it themselves!

Hand ups are important at school. Too often kids don't ask for help with assignments or subjects they don't understand. They're afraid that they'll seem stupid. They don't want to embarrass themselves in front of their friends or teachers they admire. So send the teacher a quick e-mail anytime your child expresses hesitation about getting help at school. When the teacher makes the first move, it can really take the pressure off. Make sure your kids understand that getting academic help is a hand up, not a handout!

Hand ups can be very useful lessons inside the home. When a child is overwhelmed by homework and truly needs help getting their chores done, asking for help is a hand up for their academic efforts. Getting a ride to a special event from a friend or a neighbor should be repaid with a thank-you note or some other gesture that helps the friend, because a hand up helps your child grow; hand ups help everyone!

MARK MILESTONES

Mark milestones to help your child recognize how much their achievements count.

Marking milestones enhances your child's self-esteem. It also strengthens their personalities and identities by letting them know that teachers and parents aren't the only ones paying attention to their achievements. They realize early on that the world is much bigger!

Mark milestones in your child's academic life. The beginning and ending of each school year is a great time to hold a special event with your child's friends. Every grading period can be celebrated for its successes. In between, smaller milestones like boosting a test score or finishing extra credit assignments are also worth noticing. At the beginning of the year, ask teachers for a quick overview of the milestones they'll want the students to make. When you mark the same milestones as your child's teacher, the message about the importance of education is received loud and clear!

Mark milestones in other areas of your child's life. Take pictures of things you do together as a family, like vacations or going for a hike. Set up a logbook of their extracurricular activities and note statistics like you would for a sports team. Dedicate a calendar to a hobby your child is learning and color in days when they learn a new skill. Mark the milestones and you'll support their growth every step of the way!

SELF-RELIANCE

Self-reliance is a skill that will take your child through the little issues and even the unthinkable ones.

Self-reliance is a critical skill for every child to learn. They will reach different levels of independence as they grow, which prepares them for the next level. They will become more responsible for everything from schoolwork to their health. They will even become more mature and look out for others!

Self-reliance is an important skill for learning. Every time the teacher hands out an assignment, students need to tackle that task on their own. They need the strength of will to persist even when the task is difficult, and they need to understand enough about themselves to know that they can finish what they have started. And remember that kids often act differently in school than they do at home. Check in with the teacher every few months to ensure that your child is a self-reliant student. Self-reliance builds learners who succeed!

Self-reliance is especially important within the family. You don't always have time to tend to your child's every tiny need. Each kid needs to be able to handle a certain amount of their own needs so that the entire family can remain balanced and healthy. And, if the worst happens and you are suddenly no longer in their lives, they need the skills to survive without you. Teaching self-reliance is one of the most loving things a parent can do.

CAMP OUT

Camping out engages the entire family in different kinds of nature trips.

Camp out to support your child's intellectual, emotional, social, and physical development. You'll find that they're immediately more creative when they're outdoors. They'll be curious and explore, even if they're old enough to want to hide the fact that they're exploring!

Camp out at school to help your child de-stress during the school day. Whenever the weather promises to be nice, send them off with a note in their backpack reminding them to look out a window between classes. Encourage them to eat lunch outside. If you live in a climate that isn't nice much of the school year, set up a drive to donate potted plants for the school's halls and common spaces. That little touch of nature means a lot!

Camp out by engaging in outdoor activities with the entire family. Go on a camping trip, even if it's only for one night. Pack everyone in the car and find a hiking trail for a day trip. Pack a picnic lunch and eat on your front lawn or your balcony! If all else fails, put up posters of landscapes in your child's room and in the living room and kitchen.

Studies have found that looking at landscape pictures for as little as sixty seconds can de-stress and relax our minds.

COMMON COMFORT

Common comfort provides regular soothing for the tough times.

Common comfort builds a sense of trust with your child. When you provide comfort for all the little issues that crop up every day, your kids automatically turn to you when really bad things happen. Since they have that trust in you, you'll be able to help them much more effectively.

Common comfort applies to school! Your child spends much of their waking time at school every week, so the little things that crop up there should be something you provide comfort for regularly. Always make sure that their teacher knows they can call, text, e-mail, or send a note home. They can often spot the need for comforting because they interact on a very different level with your child. Then, when a subject gets really difficult or a bully threatens, your child will be much more likely to ask for help right away. That allows you both to tackle the issue before it really gets out of hand.

Common comfort works best when it happens inside the home. Whenever you comfort someone else, they need to open up and be vulnerable. To truly offer comfort, the environment needs to be safe. By offering comfort inside the home regularly, you'll enable your child to seek and accept comfort from you in other locations, and under very different circumstances.

CHASE DREAMS

Chase dreams with your kids to help them envision big things for their lives!

Chasing dreams with your children helps them develop judgment. Knowing that an adult values their goals enhances their self-esteem. They also get to practice reaching high—under the safe umbrella of your guidance!

Chasing dreams at school sets children up as lifelong learners. If their dearest wish is to work on the school newspaper, help them learn how to take pictures or research articles. When they discover a subject they really enjoy, find groups in the school or after school that focus on that topic. Include the school's teachers in this loop. They're the ones who know what's coming in the future, so they will provide you with guidance on all the opportunities!

Chase dreams with your child even if they seem unattainable or silly. Your youngest child might not have the judgment they need to realize when something is out of their reach. Use your adult judgment to help them create that dream in a different way. Not every child can travel to outer space. Every child can visit a science museum, go to space camp, and travel the stars with online documentaries. Chase any part of that dream and you'll bring it to life!

RESERVE JUDGMENT

Reserve judgment until you have all the facts.

Reserving judgment provides your child with balanced authority. They will trust you to be fair even when they've done something wrong. That trust is important because if things go really bad, they need to be able to come to you for help. Reserve judgment until you are certain you know all the facts and can judge appropriately.

Reserve judgment about school-related issues. If your child proclaims that the new teacher is mean, ask why they think that. Find out exactly what the teacher did or said to trigger that response in your child. Then you'll know if the teacher is actually mean, just a little grumpy, or whether your child is having other problems and has focused on the teacher instead of trying to fix the real problem.

Reserve judgment by maintaining control over your emotions. Every person, and especially a parent, has a fight-or-flight response. When you hear a piece of news that doesn't sound good, you're naturally going to feel angry or afraid or frustrated—and sometimes all three! Recognize that the response is normal and natural. Take a deep breath, push back at that emotion, and then use your logical mind to gather all the facts.

SETTLE SEX

Settle sex questions by providing age-appropriate information regularly.

Settle sex by giving your children the information they need when they need it. At a very young age, they're going to wonder where babies come from. Later, they're going to think they know all about where babies come from! Keep them properly informed to keep them safe from disease and unwanted responsibilities.

When you *settle sex* for your children, you help them navigate the social world of school. You ensure that they understand what appropriate touching is so that they're never vulnerable to predators. And you keep them aware of how their hugs or touches might not be welcomed by other kids in their classroom. Teachers can be a big help here, too, and not just through sex-education programs! Ask to be alerted to anything that seems inappropriate or uncomfortable about the situations your child steps into. Together, you'll keep your kids safe!

Settle sex by assessing what your child is ready for at every age. Provide them with books and videos that present what you want them to know at that time. And don't think that if you don't give it to them they will stay ignorant! They'll hear strange tales from friends and stumble across things they don't understand on TV and the Internet. Make sure they know that they can always ask you by providing them with the information they need.

EMPHASIZE EDUCATION

Emphasize education in your home to support your child's best at school.

A strong home *emphasizes education.* A parent's concern and involvement has been shown to enhance academic performance. When your home is set up to support education, your child has a much easier pathway day by day, which makes the path easier over the years!

Emphasize education by connecting the home environment directly to school activities. Every child should have a desk or other dedicated study area. The area should be quiet for those who need silence to study. It might be in the kitchen for kids who focus best when there is a lot of background noise. You know your kids best, so set up the environment that connects them to school!

A study in the *Review of Economics and Statistics* reported that *emphasizing education* in the home has a bigger impact on a child's success than anything a teacher does. It's even more important than the effort the student expends! All the things discussed in this book—reading aloud, volunteering at the school, attending teacher-parent meetings— are ways to highlight your commitment to your child's education.

HANDLE HEALTH

Handle health by monitoring wellness and addressing any issues early. *Handling health* ensures that your children live each day in the best possible physical condition. Small ailments like a cold or flu can leave them vulnerable to other illnesses. Being tired or overwhelmed can lead to short-term sickness, which can then lead to long-term health issues. Make being well a daily priority and you'll energize your child's body and their mind!

Handle health issues related to school attendance. Every day, your child goes into a building with hundreds or even thousands of other people. The desktops might not have been cleaned for a while, and keyboards and other equipment will have been touched by many hands between cleanings. Teach your children good hygiene habits like hand washing to keep them healthy at school. Ask your child's teacher if you can send a bottle of hand sanitizer to the classroom for everyone to use. If not, find a cartoon about hygiene and ask the teacher to share it with the whole class.

Handle health in the home by providing nourishing meals and insisting on exercise. Make sure your kids know how to snack in a healthy way on fruits and half-sized portions of chips or candy. Fresh air, sunshine, activity outdoors, and other simple steps keep your kids healthy. And if they complain about a stomach ache or a headache, make sure it's not the start of something bigger before you send them off to school.

CATCH THE GOOD

Catch the good lets you reward children for doing well!

Catch the good helps to counteract all the time you catch your kids being bad. When you're constantly telling them no, you become only an authoritarian in their eyes. By "catching" them doing something right, you develop a relationship that goes far beyond leader and follower. You become a loving parent-child team!

Catch the good at school. Ask your child's teachers to send you an e-mail once in a while when your child performs especially well. They might help another student without being asked or really take a leap forward with their studies. As always, check in with your child's teacher on this. They see a lot of things that you'll never know about because you aren't there. When you're in the know, you can catch your child doing well and praise them the same day it happens.

Catch the good at home and in public places. Parents can get so overworked that they collapse on the couch at the end of the day. As long as the house is quiet, they leave the kids alone. But that's usually the time when you can catch them doing something good! Notice when your child is especially quiet or managing their emotions and chores. Don't wait for them to report back to you. Catch them in the act so they know you're always paying attention!

CRYSTAL CLEAR

Crystal clear communications help your child stay within the boundaries you have set.

Crystal clear communications ease daily life for you and your child. Understanding the rules helps your child know what you expect. Knowing exactly where the boundaries are allows your kids to steer clear of them. And when they grow enough to want to challenge those boundaries, they will be well aware of the fact that they need to communicate with you!

Crystal clear communications help your child's academic performance. When you have open channels of communication, your child knows they can ask for help, talk things over, and use you to guide them toward clarity on the issues that seem very complex to them. With you by their side, they have a lot more energy to apply to academic success.

Be *crystal clear* about the behaviors you expect within your family. Inside the house, you might allow for a lot more freedom in what your kids do and say. Outside the house or when guests arrive, a different set of rules might govern where they're allowed to play and how they can participate in conversations. Let your kids know over time how those rules change to reflect their growing maturity. You'll help them mature much more quickly than if they're never sure what the rules are!

LOVE AND LOGIC

Love and logic in equal parts keeps your parenting in balance!

Love and logic is about using all the best skills you have as a parent. Your love is a self-evident skill you can call on in good times and bad. Your logic is based on your knowledge and wisdom, and also helps in a variety of situations. When you balance the two in every decision, you create the best parenting possible!

Love and logic works for schoolwork! A love of education might not be something you can inspire in your child, but you can certainly discover what brings them pleasure. Encourage them to explore subjects in fun ways outside school. Download movies or visit places associated with history, and you might spark a love for the subject that encourages your child to apply themselves more. Ask the teachers for copies of their lesson plans at the beginning of the year and plan activities around those lessons. Then you've used your logic to inspire their love!

Strike the balance between *love and logic* every time you interact with your child. When they ask for permission to do something, check that your initial response isn't overwhelmed by a loving desire to keep them safe. Ask yourself if participating in this activity could help your child grow or challenge them in a new way. If they can handle that, guide your child through the love/logic process by asking them to share what they think they will get out of the experience. Then make your decision in a balanced way!

CREATE COMMANDMENTS

Create commandments that everyone in your house follows for life!

Creating commandments lays out positive expectations for your child's behavior and for their growth. When everyone in the house is held to the same commandments, your kids recognize that they are never to be breached. Commandments provide a strong way to introduce values that your children will hold for their lifetimes.

Create commandments around academic efforts. They might include the following: *Always try your best, ask for help,* and *respect your work.* When kids try their best, they know they will succeed no matter what the outcome. Asking for help sets them up to receive assistance in a positive way. When they respect their own work, they are much less likely to allow others to pressure them into providing answers for students who are lazy.

Create commandments for your household. Your family's commandments might be: *Respect yourself, love your brothers and sisters,* and *stand up for what you believe in.* List the commandments in a prominent place or set them up as screensavers on your kid's computer. When a situation arises that demonstrates the importance of one or more of the commandments, discuss it with your child. You'll emphasize the importance of all the commandments and provide a new way to look at something they already know.

SHOUT A SLOGAN

Shout a slogan to boost your child's morale.

When you *shout a slogan,* you share a moment with your child that is deeply imbued with meaning. You have created the slogan together, so the words represent a conversation you two have had about good things and positive feelings. Every repetition of the slogan triggers those same positive feelings!

Shout a slogan associated with schoolwork. Help your child set a slogan for their schoolwork in general or have different ones associated with different topics. They might be as varied as *Master math* to encourage attention in a difficult subject or *History is happy* to emphasize the attraction a certain topic has for your child. If you have more than one child, help each one create their own slogan! A quick e-mail to the teacher will ensure that the slogan is repeated throughout the day. And you just might start a trend that helps the entire class!

Every family should have a *slogan they can shout.* Your family might choose *All for one and one for all* to emphasize that no matter what happens, you are all in it together. If siblings are constantly fussing at each other, you might opt for *Love is peaceful, love is kind.* Every time your family hits a crisis point, shouting the slogan together will boost their morale. Be sure to shout it during the happy times, too! It will enhance the positive feelings every time.

LET THEM QUIT

Let them quit because sometimes kids need to try things to find out that it's not the right fit!

Letting them quit provides your children with the ability to make decisions for themselves. When they know that they will be able to step away from an obligation if they have good reasons, they become more willing to try new things. Letting them quit recognizes their ability to be responsible for their own judgment.

Let them quit certain things related to school. Your child should always be able to withdraw from an extracurricular activity, if they don't have time for it or if they simply don't like it. If they are really struggling with a subject, you might let them quit that level of academic engagement by shifting them to a different class. Once they're engaged in a level of learning that fits their abilities, they'll be able to advance at their own speed.

Let them quit activities they absolutely hate through tradeoffs. If they are really resistant to a particular chore and there's no benefit to forcing them to perform the chore, ask them what they are willing to trade to get out of that chore. They might be willing to do twice as much work on a different chore, or they might cut their own allowance to be released from that dreaded duty. You don't have to let them quit every time, but if it works out well for your entire family, make it happen!

BREAK TIME

A *break time* can help kids at every age.

Break time gives your kids a minute (or more) to unwind and de-stress. Their world demands a lot from them, and they're learning new things every day. Giving them break time allows their minds to refresh. If you take the break alongside them, then you'll both benefit!

Break time from academic work is important! When your child comes home from school, remember that they've been working hard all day and meeting the demands of many adults. If you start laying out the chore list or fussing about where they've set their backpack, it might be the final straw. Avoid meltdowns at any age by giving your child five minutes to decompress after they get home. If you think break time would be good during the school day, ask your child's teacher if there's a way to integrate one minute of silence or a short chant like "Good, better, best!" to recharge the students. Since we all need a break, the teachers might find that it helps them, too!

Break time can be valuable whenever you see things heading downhill. When a child is grumpy or depressed, make sure they have five minutes to themselves before you ask what happened. During school holidays, make sure they get a long break away from academic work by scheduling fun activities. The more you join in the fun, the more your entire family will benefit from break time!

TEE UP TRADITIONS

Tee up traditions to forge a strong family unit.

Tee up traditions with your kids to provide them with a sense of family history. At first you'll develop all the traditions. As your kids grow, they can think up traditions they would like the family to be involved in. Have a meeting once a year to add a tradition to your list, and you'll always be growing as a unit!

Tee up traditions around school schedules. You might have a back-to-school party two weeks before school opens. Invite your child's friends and their parents so that the adults can have fun, too! You'll help your child strengthen old friendships while you build new connections among other parents at your school.

Tee up traditions by noticing what makes your family special. Make an annual sojourn back to the place where you were born or where your own parents came from. Mark the unique holidays associated with your child's skills like National Science Day or National Poetry Day by engaging in something related to those skills on those days. Have fun teeing up traditions, and you'll build a special world for your children!

MINGLE MESSAGES

Mingle messages on a central board to enhance communication and develop a sense of togetherness!

When you *mingle messages*, you allow your entire family to know where everyone is at any moment. It gives children a feeling of comfort and safety to know where you are at every moment of your day. You'll feel the same comfort and security of knowing where your kids are!

Mingle messages about school on your family's board. This keeps everyone informed about special events, milestones achieved, and successes that have come along. Kids will be inspired by their siblings' accomplishments and try harder at their own studies. When school messages are mixed on the regular family message board, your kids will know that education is as much a natural part of their day as your job is for you.

Mingle messages for the entire family in one place. When you set up a central whiteboard where everyone can make notes, you allow the family to easily keep up with each other. Color code the messages so that everyone knows red is from one parent, green is from the oldest son, and so on. At random times, you can post positive sayings or quirky pictures to make checking the board fun!

ONE WORD

One word can speak volumes.

One word can have a much greater impact on your kids than a long lecture. When you talk and talk and talk, they are very likely just to tune you out and wait until you're done. Use one carefully selected word, though, and they'll get your message—fast!

One word can work with schoolwork. When your child wants to go out and play, say, "Homework." The message is clear: Once the work is done, then comes playtime. Since you haven't said anything other than one word, there isn't anything to argue about or use as an excuse. Let your child's teacher in on this, too. There's every reason to start this kind of habit with the entire class!

One word makes your home life much easier. You know by now the kinds of situations you're going to encounter again and again. Before the next occurrence, find the single word that conveys your usual message. If your teenager is heading out the door, you might call, "Curfew!" When your youngster starts another tantrum, try repeating "calm" until they actually do calm down. When you don't offer anything else, they realize they're going to have to follow along if they want to get anywhere!

HARNESS HABITS

Harness habits your child has to serve you and your family.

When you *harness habits,* you ease the pressure on a child to change parts of their personality that are core to their being. You eliminate any message that might whisper that they aren't good enough. Instead, you find a way to use that same habit in a positive, powerful way.

Harness habits to enhance your child's education. If your youngest is always up before the sun, that might be the best time for that child to do homework. Teenagers who don't start to wake up until after noon might work best after a short break when they come home. You can't change these things about your kids but you can harness them!

Harness habits associated with other areas of family and home life. If your child is a very slow eater, don't rush them through a meal for any reason. Instead, add extra time if you are heading out somewhere after a meal. Use the extra few minutes to chat with the other family members who have finished eating. Then everyone can feel more connected!

Part II

Trusted Knowledge for Yourself

LOVE HAS A VOICE

Love has a voice that should be lifted daily.

Love has a voice that should never be silenced. Parents who withhold affection raise children who are stunted emotionally. Parents who don't know how to show their love raise children who can't find friends and who are abandoned by the few friends they do find. Love isn't rocket science. Even your dog is capable of love!

Love has a voice that doesn't have to speak with words. Love is demonstrated by the time you spend at work so there is enough money to pay the bills. It is felt in the gentle touch or the reassuring squeeze to a child's arm. Love is the smile that lights up your face whenever you see your kids, and it sings in the laughter that you create inside your home. Lift the voice of love every day!

Your children know that *love has a voice*, and they are waiting to hear it. Not from friends or neighbors or distant relatives, or even the heartthrob of the week. They are hungry to hear the voice of love that rises from your heart. Touch them. Smile at them. Tell them you are proud of them, and help them through the tough spots. If you don't, that hunger will drive them to other sources. They'll have sex long before they're ready. They'll drink or do drugs to soothe the pain in their hearts. They'll do stupid things just to feel the rush of danger because something very important is missing. Speak with the voice of love and your children will never starve.

MODEL YOUR BEST

Model your best so that your kids have a guide they trust on their road through life.

Modeling your best provides you with two very important benefits. First, it gives your children an adult to look up to. Second, it proves that you don't ask for anything you're not willing to do yourself! When you model your best, your kids will trust that you practice what you preach. They'll know you expect the best from them—and yourself.

You don't have a choice about *modeling your best.* The fact that you are a parent means that your kids will look to you for guidance. They might never ask for it directly, but they're watching you all the time! Every word you speak and every action you undertake are being studied and dissected. Be sure to ask the school's teachers about the social and emotional lessons they have integrated into the classroom. When you ask those kinds of questions, you're more likely to hear about kids—and even other parents—your child should avoid. Whenever any adult in their lives gives less than their best, they are modeling a slacker attitude for your kids.

Model your best means that you're going to have to pay attention to your manners! Don't answer your phone at the dinner table. Keep promises to your kids, your family, and everyone else. Have a set of values that are your guides to everyday life. Trust in a higher power and turn to that power when you're in need—and when you're feeling grateful. Most important of all, model consistency. If you change your mind about something, don't say, "Because I said so." Explain to your kids why you changed your mind. They'll learn that it's good to be flexible and change as the circumstances change!

DOING IS TEACHING

Doing is teaching because kids mimic your every action, good and bad.

Doing is teaching goes further than being a role model. It means that you can show your kids the healthiest way to live! By eating good food in the right amounts, you teach them that healthy food is their body's foundation. When you take only the medications prescribed for you, you teach them that drugs are tools for healing.

Doing is teaching at a very early age. One-year-olds copy their parents to learn about the world. A study done with kids aged two through six found that when allowed to shop in a store with miniature replicas of food and products, 28 percent of the kids bought cigarettes and 61 percent bought alcohol. If they think it's important enough to buy, they will soon think it's important enough to use! Check in with your child's teachers to find out what's going on at the school. If there's a lot of graffiti on the buildings surrounding the campus or older kids are acting up, you'll know what kinds of things to talk to your kids about before they think it's cool to copy.

Doing is teaching at every age! Kids don't stop learning from you just because they turn five or twelve or eighteen. If you're constantly dieting to lose "just a few pounds," your kids might turn to their own perfect bodies and wonder if they should do the same. The type of television shows you watch, the way you treat your friends and neighbors, and how you deal with pressure are absorbed by your sons and daughters. Do them a huge favor and teach by doing what's right.

LIES ARE LIES

Lies are lies no matter how you try to justify them.

Lies are lies, and all lies are harmful. The little white lies you tell to save someone's feelings still aren't true. Lying to your kids to get through the moment doesn't make your life easier, and it might really hurt them. Asking your kids to lie for you so you can get around a rule puts them in a horrible situation. And it teaches them that lying is OK!

Lies are lies because they hurt your kids. Threats that a monster will grab them if they don't behave make them scared of the unknown. Lying about when something will happen is a promise you know you're going to break, which makes your kids lose trust in you. Covering up reality presents things in the wrong light and makes them question your wisdom. Keep your children close by telling them the truth!

Lies are lies but boy, are little white ones convenient. Take the high road. Yes, you'll have to climb higher and work harder. But your kids are worth it. When your daughter wears a new outfit that's totally wrong for her, either gently ask if she wants advice on selecting clothes or keep your mouth shut. When your son keeps failing at a sport he's clearly not capable of performing, either ask if he would like to try a different sport or keep your mouth shut! Think about how to help. Don't sugarcoat the world and you'll raise kids who are better prepared for reality.

BAN THREATS

Ban threats because they're all destructive.

Ban threats that make your kids scared of you or that are idle and meaningless to begin with. Provide information instead, and your kids will learn the real consequences to their actions and be empowered to avoid them. You'll start building the wisdom they need to correctly assess how what they do today can affect them tomorrow. And you'll build a relationship based on trust.

Ban the threats that can cause the most damage to young minds. When it's time to go and your child just won't cooperate, don't say that you'll leave them behind. The threat triggers fears of being abandoned and shakes their security in the entire family structure. Make sure your child's teachers are on board. If they tell your kid there's a consequence for not doing homework, make it clear that you want your child to know that the consequence really will happen! Stay in charge and stay in command. Don't tell them you're going to stop being the parent by leaving them behind!

For young kids, *ban threats* and replace them with specific guidance. Tell them exactly what you want them to do. Break it down into small steps they can easily understand and follow. As your children grow older, you can add explanations. Tell them why they should do things a certain way as well as the consequences of not following along. You'll guide their judgments and wisdom every day!

HUGS ARE FREE

Hugs are free, so give them freely!

Hugs are free, yet they return so much! They convey how much you love your kids. Your children feel secure in the strength of your affection. Hugs can relieve the stress your kids feel and boost their immune system. Best of all, hugs make you both happy!

Hugs are free, but some parents must think they cost a lot because they rarely offer any. If this sounds like you, figure out why you're so stingy. Did you come from a family that didn't support you or value you? Do you think you're too busy to stop for a moment? Or have you relegated all the childcare to your spouse or a different family member? Whatever the problem, eliminate it. Throw out those old ways and give your kid a hug right now!

Hugs are free and are so easy to give. Some kids have developmental issues that make them resistant to physical touch. Sometimes children are too upset to accept a hug. Keep these things in mind when you offer one. Make sure your touch is gentle, and let the firmness grow gradually if that's appropriate. Never use a hug as a way to trap a child physically so you can tickle or tease them; you'll only destroy their trust. Keep your heart as open as your arms, and your hugs will be delicious!

JOIN THE PTA

Join the PTA (Parent Teacher Association), to help yourself and your child!

Join the PTA to discover all the resources they can offer parents with school-age kids. You'll access a huge network of other parents who can support you. The professionals you'll encounter there might have exactly the answer you're looking for. You'll also be able to help at your local school, which benefits your entire community.

Joining the PTA is easy. With over 20,000 groups around the country, the PTA is where you need it to be! Through them, you'll make your voice heard with your school administrators, your child's teachers, and even your local and national politicians. The best part is that you'll have plenty of opportunities to engage with the teachers. Look ahead a year or two and talk to teachers in the next grade level. Then you'll be prepared to help your child prepare for the next academic year. Plus, you'll be fully connected to your school and know everything that goes on there, even when your kid forgets to tell you things!

Join the PTA with the fullness of your heart and your efforts. Commit to volunteering for one thing every year through the group. Even if you're very busy, you can help stuff envelopes one night or contribute an article to their newsletter. Every time you help out, you'll move deeper into the network of other parents and educators. You'll benefit as much as your kids!

KILL THE KARAOKE

Kill the karaoke means try not to embarrass your kids!

Kill the karaoke so that your kids won't be embarrassed to greet you or be seen with you. In a recent survey—conducted by Comedy Central

UK, of all places, which proves how absurd this whole parenting thing can be—71 percent of preteens and teens said they often felt embarrassed by their parents. Over 15 percent were so mortified they refused to let their parents pick them up after school and other events! The more you embarrass them, the fewer chances you'll have to spend time together and strengthen your bond.

Kill the karaoke around school activities. You need to be able to show up at school for a lot of reasons: to meet with teachers, to bring up issues with the principal, even just to volunteer your time. Every time you visit, you have another opportunity to see how your child behaves in school and around their peers. If they're too busy trying to hide because you embarrass them, you'll miss your chance to learn something new.

Kill the karaoke by considering the top reasons kids are embarrassed by their parents. If kissing or cuddling them in public makes them uncomfortable, save that for when you're at home. Don't tell stories about when they were younger. Don't criticize them in public. Don't use their baby nicknames after they've outgrown them. And don't whip out the baby photos if they're old enough to go to school!

ONE VOICE

Speak with *one voice* as parents, even if you are the only parent in the home!

Speaking with *one voice* keeps your kids on track. When you and your spouse work out the details before you talk to your kids, you present them with a united front that can't be breached. Tell the teacher that they are the one voice your child should follow during the school day. And when you're the only parent in the home, you are the singular voice that holds authority—above your kid's grandparent or neighbor, above their teacher!

The authority of *one voice* helps your kids navigate school. First, you've very clearly laid out your expectations for their education, so they know that they are in school for only one thing. The friends they meet and the other activities they enjoy are bonuses, not the reason they go to school! Second, and just as important, the authority of your singular voice helps your kids handle peer pressure and stay out of trouble! Third, when their teacher is the one voice they need to heed during the day, they don't have to wonder who to turn to for advice.

Speaking with *one voice* is one of the best things you can do for your kids. If you and your spouse disagree on something, talk it over in private. Make sure you both present what you see as the benefits and drawbacks of each option, so that both of you have the same information and perspective. Then find a midpoint on which you can both agree. The same goes if you're a single parent and you need help from a family member, a neighbor, or a caregiver. Make sure the person who is helping you knows what you want to happen!

NO MEANS NO

When *no means no*, you set boundaries in which your child can truly be free!

No means no sounds very negative but, when applied correctly, is very positive for you and your child. Once you've made a decision, you bolster your own authority by holding on to that decision. Children who know where the boundaries lie are free to explore within those boundaries. And they feel safe because your decision isn't going to change!

When *no means no* at home, it helps your child manage their days at school. They recognize that adults hold positions of authority, and they are more likely to follow the rules when you're not around. And when you've said no to an activity that could be pursued during the school day, send the teacher a quick note to let them know it's off limits! Knowing that no always means no helps your child make decisions based on your guidance and wisdom.

One of the toughest things can be to make *no mean no.* You want to reward your child and make them feel loved. You also want to take time off every now and then from all your responsibilities! Providing kids with a stable authority is one of the best ways you can prove your love. And when you need time off, do it on your own time, not your child's!

BE DEMOCRATIC

Being democratic allows your child to have a say in some things.

Be democratic to fully instill a sense of ownership in your child. When kids have a say in what they do or how they do it, they take the task seriously. Their sense of responsibility grows, and they recognize that their responsibilities will increase as they get older.

Be democratic with school decisions. The youngest children can pick the colors of the pencils they will use when it's time to buy school supplies. Grade schoolers can be responsible for selecting the clothes they wear to school. Preteens in junior high can decide which after-school activities they want to join, while those in high school might determine whether they're going to work after school or on the weekends. To make school activities fully democratic, invite your child's teacher to chime in with their opinion. Your kid will benefit by hearing from different adults and will be better prepared to make sound decisions.

Being democratic is an age-appropriate activity. As your child grows, the types of decisions you allow them to participate in will change. The amount of responsibility you give them for each decision will change, too. If you're unsure whether to hand over responsibility on a particular task, consider what might happen if things go wrong. Will you be able to clean up the fallout? Will working through the failure help your child grow? If the answer to both is yes, go ahead and give them the vote!

SLEEPOVERS ARE SERIOUS

Sleepovers are serious fun that require a parent's serious judgment.

When *sleepovers are serious*, the adults have taken every precaution to keep a herd of rambunctious kids safe. And as our world rolls on, the age at which kids can get into serious trouble gets younger and younger. Remembering that sleepovers aren't a night off for the parents keeps the focus where it needs to be.

Sleepovers are serious because they can actually help at school! Your child can build friendships during sleepovers in ways that just can't be done during the busy school day. When new kids at school invite classmates to sleepovers, the time together can help them meet new people and figure out if they want to be close friends. You can even have sleepovers when kids are working on group projects to give them time to brainstorm or build something together.

Sleepovers are serious for parents. A lot of work is involved in getting the house ready and making sure there's food to go around. More than that, though, the parent has to make a lot of serious decisions. Are the kids on the invitation list allowed at your house? Will the group sleep in a bedroom behind a closed door or will they pile into the living room? Is a second adult available in case one of the kids needs to be taken home? All this assumes the sleepover is at your house. If your child wants to attend a sleepover at someone else's house, you have a whole different set of responsibilities.

MAKE MEMORIES

Make memoires that will last for your child's lifetime.

Making memories builds a treasure trove that no one can ever steal from your child. You'll be able to recreate the same types of experiences you had as a child and provide your own child with entirely new experiences. Believe me when I tell you that those same memories will be shared with their children—and their children's children.

Making memories helps your child navigate the social and academic world of school. When children have a strong family as their foundation, they are able to say no to peer pressure. Children who have a sense of their own personal history are much more likely to strive to do well. They are able to look forward to their own future because they recognize that there is more to their world than just this present moment.

Making memories is something you're already doing! Every time you spend time with your children—time focused on your children, not your electronic device or your work problems—you are creating memories of love and affection. Cement those special feelings in their hearts by playing with them in the yard or going for walks around the neighborhood to share a chat or just to walk in silence. The special times are moments when neither of you is busy with something. Clear space to build clear memories!

LOVE IS EQUAL

Love is equal because it doesn't play favorites.

Love is equal in every household. When children know that they are as beloved as their brothers and sisters, their sense of self is supported. Loving them equally allows you to treat each as an individual without causing rifts between siblings, or between your children and yourself.

Love is equal when it comes to your child's education. Each child should receive the same opportunities that relate to his schooling. If one was allowed to go on a special trip or engage in extracurricular activities, the others should be allowed the same freedoms. Alert teachers about this, too. It can be tough to have things balanced at home only to have them be unbalanced (or appear to be unbalanced) at school. No child should ever feel that his education is less important than that of his siblings because they're younger, a different gender, or for any other reason. *Love is equal* in the home. Every one of your children should have a special time set aside just for them every week. If there are two parents in the home, the second parent can spend time alone with the same child on alternating weeks. What you do during that time doesn't matter. It does matter that the same amount of time is devoted to each child. Let the child decide whether to go somewhere, play in the yard, or just talk!

PRAY LARGE

Pray large for your kids to take them through the toughest times.

Praying large is all about bringing your spiritual values to bear on the life of your children. When they're facing peer pressure, health issues, or other big troubles, they need you to pray in a big way for them. Their issues loom large, so their needs are equally large!

Praying large helps your kids with the worst issues they'll face at school. Bullying can go far beyond a few taunts and drive kids into depression or to consider suicide. Learning difficulties can keep your children from advancing as quickly, and make them feel like they're being left behind by their friends. Focus your spiritual efforts and prayerful thoughts on these issues to pray large!

Pray large by being clear about the issue and the result you'd like to see. When bullying is the issue, you might focus on providing your child with a safe environment where the bully can't reach. That can range from removing the bully to implementing a change of heart in the bully. Both of those are really big goals! But they're the point of praying large. Hoping that your child can cope isn't going to make the issue go away. Removing the bully or changing the environment will.

RIDE HERD

Ride herd on your kids by keeping watch on everything they do!

Riding herd on your kids keeps them safe and happy and healthy. When you know exactly what they're up to every minute, you know whether you can allow them to continue or whether you need to step in. And because you're able to intervene early, you can work with your kids to help them decide when to turn away from a particular activity for their own good!

Ride herd over your children's education. Make sure homework assignments are completed in full and on time. Encourage them to participate in extracurricular activities, especially those that teach skills that aren't offered in the regular class selections. Ask your kids how they spent their day every day. And if something sounds a little off, don't hesitate to ask the child's teacher for their perspective. You'll begin to know exactly when they're trying to hide something, so you'll be able to take action early if something isn't going well.

Ride herd over the areas where your kids might stumble into danger. That includes their Internet surfing activity, the TV shows they download, and the movies they attend with friends. Try Footprints, an app that shows you on a map where your kids have gone during the day. TeenSafe is an app that allows you to monitor text messages, web browsing, call logs, and even social media feeds. Ride herd over the danger spots to keep your kids safe!

PRACTICE PATIENCE

Practice patience by remembering that your kids are—well, kids!

Practicing patience works wonders with your kids. It lets them know that you're always going to remain a balanced and stable force in their lives. They know that if you get angry, they need to pay full attention because you don't get angry over nothing. And since patience helps you stay calm, it's great for you, too!

Practice patience with your child's school assignments. At times, you'll find that you need the homework to be done so you can do something special with your child. Or the struggles that they're experiencing at school are coming home with them and making meals less than enjoyable. Call on your empathy in these situations. Recognize that the learning process takes time. And remember how tough simple things seemed to you at that age!

Practice patience when you know that bad behavior is linked to something else. Maybe they didn't sleep well the night before or they haven't eaten on time, so they're hungry. If their bad behavior is linked to that, know that it's not really their fault. And when poor behavior is their fault, practice additional patience! By staying calm, you'll be able to manage the poor behavior in the best possible way.

OPEN WIDE

Open wide reminds you to keep an open mind about your child's goals and dreams!

When you are *open wide*, you are ready to allow your child to be and do whatever they need to become a unique individual. Open-minded parents raise children who know who they are, and who love themselves just the way they are. They find that their kids strive more and even achieve more!

Open wide around school-based activities. When your child talks about new concepts that don't sound like something you want them exposed to, ask for more information. And don't just rely on your child, who might not be mature enough to explain things properly. Go to the school's web site to learn more or make a quick call to their teacher. If you have to, call the school's office and ask for information. An open mind ensures that your child is allowed to explore.

Open wide in all areas of your child's life. Adjust your perspective so that you can remember what it was like to explore the world at their age. Certain things that aren't great ideas can look very appealing. Whenever possible, allow your child to explore those things enough to discover that they don't want to go there! Keep your hand in theirs, and together you'll ensure that an open mind finds all the right answers.

HOMEGROWN CONFERENCE

Homegrown conferences allow your entire family to work together to make decisions.

Homegrown conferences build a sense of self-esteem in your kids. Even if they aren't old enough to vote on a particular issue, they can provide their opinions about things the family is considering. That alone empowers them on a level other kids never even hear about!

Homegrown conferences can address educational issues and academic success. In certain years, your children will have the opportunity to select certain types of classes. Nearly every year, they'll have the chance to participate in special events and extracurricular activities. They should bring those choices to the family conference. When you know what's on the docket, you can call the teachers to discuss the details. Then you'll know exactly what the benefits might be as well as what the child or your family might have to trade off for that opportunity. The student's activities will impact everyone who wants to attend or support them, so it should be on the docket for discussion!

Homegrown conferences build unity within your family. They encourage kids to speak their minds—meaning they have to think through what they want to say. Help them prepare by creating a list of points they want to make. For young kids, have them write down the one thing they think is most important to say at the meeting. As time goes on, they'll become more adept at speaking their minds. They will also learn how to listen closely to others! Both skills will help them in life, and you'll form a strong, cohesive family that makes decisions together.

WORDS HURT

Words hurt whether the bully is a classmate, a teacher, or a parent.

Words hurt kids more than adults. Children are developing their sense of identity. When the input and feedback they get is negative, they are more prone to believe negative things. And what they learn early will stick with them the rest of their lives. Support your kids with every word you speak!

Words hurt at school, so prepare your children with plenty of positive support before they even step into the kindergarten class. As they deal with mean friends, bullies, and teachers who aren't supportive, help them handle each event with supportive words and plenty of attention. Your actions will set them up for the bullies they'll meet later in life!

Words hurt in the home worst of all. If you or your spouse often speaks in anger, it's your fault! You are damaging your child in ways that will haunt them for the rest of their lives. Take yourself out of the trigger situations and learn patience. Figure out how to harness your tongue. Never tell a child that they are stupid, ugly, or worthless. Every time you do, you become small and mean in your own eyes. Stand up and do what's right for your child!

FORGET YOUR DREAMS

Forget your dreams so that you don't expect to live them through your child. *Forget your dreams* to allow your children to blossom in the way that fits them best. Everyone has regrets at some point in their life. Keeping those regrets to yourself gives your kids the freedom they need to grow. It also allows them to develop along their own pathways and in their own time. Nothing is healthier than that!

Forget your dreams in the academic realm. Your greatest regret might be that you didn't take a certain subject or graduate with honors. Those goals might not be your child's goals! Never force something onto them in regard to school. If you're not sure where to draw the line, pick up the phone! Their teacher will have a handle on their true potential, and they will welcome the chance to discuss it with you. Then you can learn how to be supportive instead of forceful. The use of force will turn them off to their own education and do a great deal of damage.

Forget your dreams as they relate to your children's friendships, the amount of time they spend in certain activities, and how well they do at sports. Those aspirations belonged to a different person. And since a lifetime has passed since you were young, the world has changed, too. The older aspirations might be so far out of sync with society now that you would hold your children back by placing that burden on them. Allow your kids to find their own dreams and follow them to new heights!

GO TO SCHOOL

Go to school by learning all you can about parenting skills.

Go to school to ensure that your parenting abilities are at the top of your class! No one is born knowing how to parent. Your parents might not have been the best, either. Give your kids the best parent possible by upgrading your knowledge and skills.

Go to school with your child to become a better parent. Whenever you attend special events, talk to other parents. The friendships you form can be a network of support and a way to learn new skills. Exposing yourself to the methods other parents use can give you new insights and change the way you think. Introduce yourself to their teachers, and when you see them again, remind them who you are and make conversation by asking about the current lesson plan or an upcoming activity. When you go to school with your child, you'll find a wealth of information!

Go to school by working a little every week on your own lesson plan. Set aside ten minutes every weekend to look up parenting skills on the Internet. You might have a specific issue you need to address that week, like how to encourage your children to do their chores. When things are going well, you can research ways to reward your children and strengthen good habits. Because the Internet can provide you with surprising links, you'll expand in ways you never knew about!

GIVE UP GOSSIP

Give up gossip around your kids to set the best example.

Give up gossip to prove to your kids that your words—and theirs— are important. Gossip destroys reputations, so when you refuse to engage in gossip, you support how deeply your children value their own reputation.

Give up gossip related to your children's school. Every time you repeat something about your children's school that you haven't confirmed is true, you break down their trust. Your kids might be young, but they need to know that the place where they spend so much time is a good place to be!

Give up gossip any time your child can hear you. Pay attention whenever you're on the phone chatting with friends. You need to gather information about rumors you have heard to protect your family. But your children don't have the same judgment or maturity as you. Make sure that doubts don't enter their minds about the rumors or about your willingness to engage in gossip! Conduct your adult conversations in private to shield your children from overhearing gossip.

CHAMPION CULTURAL SENSITIVITY

Champion cultural sensitivity to become the type of parent who raises open-minded and culturally sensitive children.

When you *champion cultural sensitivity*, you teach your kids that the world is a wide and wonderful place. You show them that there are many ways to live, all of which are valid. With the world at their fingertips, your kids will grow and expand in new directions!

Champion cultural sensitivity at your child's school. Volunteer to organize a cultural festival or a cultural celebration day. Ask all the teachers if they'd like to share stories about their backgrounds. Invite other parents to set up a table with information about their own heritage and culture. Get the kids involved by having them wear traditional clothing to the festival, and ask the teachers to do the same! Take pictures and post everything on a dedicated social media page.

Champion cultural sensitivity in your home. Every month, pick one activity for your family to share based on this value. Watch a movie or documentary about another nation. Read a story or a book about what it is like to grow up in a different country. Learn about other religious and spiritual beliefs, attend festivals, and look at artwork from other countries. You'll raise culturally aware kids and enhance your own cultural sensitivity!

FOLLOW THE PHASES

Follow the phases of parenting to ensure that your guidance always fits your child's needs.

Follow the phases of your child's life to ensure that your parenting shifts phases to match different growth cycles. You'll prevent habits from forming that keep your child stuck in immaturity. You'll lighten your own load by shifting gears and shifting more responsibility to your kids!

Follow the phases at school. Early on, your child will need you to manage much of their academic efforts. You'll even have to make sure they're getting a healthy lunch and engaging in physical activity every day. As time goes on, they can take on more responsibility. If you're unsure about when your child should be making a change, call their teacher. They deal with a lot of kids every day, so they've probably seen it all! When you are armed with the proper information, you and your child will both shift phases to make the best of each cycle.

Follow the phases by matching your efforts to your child's growth. At first you'll be the commander, the one in charge of everything. As they get a little older, you'll transform into a coach who oversees and guides. Soon you'll become a counselor who supports the decision-making process and who steps in where needed, otherwise you'll keep out!

MANAGE MODELS

Manage models because not every adult will be a good role model for your child!

When you *manage models*, you keep up with everything that's going on in your child's life. You ensure that the people they connect with are trustworthy. In the case of role models, their trustworthiness is about their value system and what they'll teach your kids.

Manage models at school by studying adults and other kids. When you visit the school, measure your child's favorite teacher by considering their approach to education and the classroom. If their discipline is lax, the teacher might be your child's favorite because the lessons are easy. Make sure your child finds a strong role model at school who will demonstrate a love of learning.

Manage models among everyone your child encounters. You might discover that one of your neighbors is attractive to your child because they live in a different way or they seem really fun to be around. That neighbor might be an alcoholic or have some other negative reason why they don't act like everyone else. Kids are drawn to unusual things and people, so be sure to keep an eye on their "new friends." You'll vet who your child emulates and keep their values intact.

FALSETTO IS FALSE

The *falsetto is false* because talking down to kids stifles young minds.

When you remember that the *falsetto is false*, you don't try to sound like a child when you talk to your children. You won't use baby talk, speak in a high voice, or dumb down what you're trying to say. You will meet them where they are—and challenge them to grow just a little bit more to keep up with you!

Falsetto is false in schoolwork. Just because your child is having a difficult time with a teacher or a subject doesn't mean the teacher is mean or the subject is tough. It might mean that your child is feeling sick or actually just doesn't like something in the classroom. Ask their teacher for advice or arrange to visit the classroom and sit quietly in the back for ten or fifteen minutes. You might be surprised that your outgoing, chatty daughter turns shy in a group or that your confident boy lets other boys bully him. Find out what's really going on and put your child back on the right path!

The *falsetto is false* at every age. Toddlers (and even younger children) who are spoken to in baby talk develop less quickly. Their slowness to communicate means they will face a host of issues, including disciplinary problems when they don't understand what you want! Set them up for a full and prosperous life right from the start. Know what they're capable of and help them grow a little bit every day by talking to them in a way that's helpful.

AVOID ABUSE

Avoid abuse by teaching your kids important safety tips.

Avoiding abuse is a necessary step for parents to take these days. When parents work hard to maintain a good home environment, children are often sent to caregiving places that are supposed to be safe but that sometimes aren't. When children know how to keep themselves safe, they can avoid abuse even when you're not there.

Avoid abuse on campus and on the way to school! Too often parents worry about the teachers and staff at a school when they really need to think about the trips their children take from home to school and back. This might be the time when they are most vulnerable. Work up a group of adults in your neighborhood who take turns meeting the bus and waiting at the stop in the mornings.

Avoid abuse wherever a child spends time. Check out the parks and playgrounds where they hang out with friends. Are busy streets within sight? That might allow a passing criminal to snatch up a spur-of-the-moment opportunity. And don't think that your front yard is safe just because you're inside the house. Check on your children frequently or enlist a neighbor to help. Invite all the neighbors to watch out for the area's kids. Adults don't have to have kids themselves to understand the need to protect them!

TAKE THE CHALLENGE

Take the challenge of parenting seriously to reap serious rewards!

Take the challenge that is parenting to heart. The job you're doing as a mother or father is filled with tough days, long nights, and the shining lights that are your children. Recognize that you're going to feel like you're pushing rocks up a hill some days. Through it all, know that when you reach the top of that hill, the view is going to be more rewarding than anything else you can do in life.

Take the challenge and parent your school-aged child in a way that supports academic success. When they flounder or can't seem to meet a challenge themselves, treat them with compassion. Find out from the teacher if their problem centers on homework, test anxiety, or only happens with certain topics. Offer comfort and then, after they've had a chance to recover their inner strength, help them face the academic challenge!

Take the challenge by being the best parent you can inside the home. The eyes of truth are always watching. Just because no one else can see your family behind closed doors doesn't give you permission to slack off. Rise to the challenge that is set before you every moment of the day. The small and large accomplishments your children make as a result will fill you with pride!

ACT, DON'T REACT

Act, don't react ensures that you're always acting in a rational and clear way.

Act, don't react prevents you from losing your cool! It helps you stay balanced in everything you do, which makes you a much better parent. When you select an action rather than responding with a reaction, you calm your own emotional response and keep the entire situation under control.

Act, don't react when things don't go well at school. When your child comes home with yet another poor grade or a negative note from the teacher, keep calm. If you need to, tell your children you need time to think and send them to their room to do homework. In fact, you can hold off on any decisions until you've talked to the teacher. Feedback from an educational professional is often exactly the thing that changes your perspective or shines a light on the issue. Then, after you've thought things through, you can engage in the right action to address the issue. *Act, don't react* by remembering first and foremost what it was like for you at your child's age. The world can be a big and scary place. New ideas and challenges pop up all the time. Kids get stressed out, too! Consider whether they are reacting rather than acting—which, given their immaturity, is very likely. Find ways to help them act instead of react and you'll both have a smoother path.

UPDATE YOUR PROGRAM

Update your program to avoid repeating what your parents did because it might not work in today's world!

Updating your program takes advantage of the latest information available from therapists, counselors, and educators. It ensures that you don't simply repeat what your parents did, because those methods might not be the best fit for today's kids. Updating your program keeps you on the cutting edge of parenting!

School is a great place to *update your program.* Make sure your children have access to whatever digital tools they need. Check to see whether your local library offers public computers and other devices. Find out if nonprofits in your area can provide or help you get the handheld devices that help with schoolwork. Use all your resources to give your children the full academic experience!

Update your program by really thinking about how you discipline your children. A generation ago, the words and actions used to ensure obedience were much harsher than what is used today. Ask yourself what you would respond to best if you were your children's age. Then find ways to implement those updated actions. Then your parenting methods will provide the best!

LEARN FROM YOUR KIDS

Learn from your kids by letting them teach you new things and new ideas!

You might be surprised to discover how much you can *learn from your kids.* We're so focused as parents on teaching them we forget they can teach us things, too! Let them change your attitude, adjust your attention, and give you the perspective they have on the world. You'll learn with the same leaps and bounds as they do!

Learn from your kids when they share their school lessons. The pace of information is so fast these days and the wealth of information available is so vast that you're sure to learn something. Sit with them when they need help and skim through their textbooks when they don't need help. Ask the teacher to send you a list of books you can read on different topics. Be sure they understand that the list is for you and not your child! You'll keep your own mind engaged and ensure that you can help when your kids need it.

Learn from your kids by tapping into their passions. When they're really struck by something and spend a lot of time doing it, ask them to teach you about it. They might love racing dirt bikes, so they can teach you how to take a corner safely. If they really enjoy a certain type of movie, your children can show you their favorite movies and tell you why they are so great. They will feel valued and respected, and you'll expand your own knowledge base at the same time!

Part III

Trusted Knowledge
for Your Outlook

HONESTY TRUMPS ALL

Just as you expect your kids to tell you the truth, *honesty trumps all* when you talk to them.

Honesty trumps all in a parent's relationship with a child. Honest parents set the best role models for their kids (and even their child's friends). Dishonesty makes children feel insecure around their parents and destabilizes the home. Honesty in the parent-child relationship strengthens the bond.

Honesty trumps all around school activities. Parents who repeatedly promise to attend special events and then don't show aren't being honest with their children or themselves. They aren't telling their kids the truth about whether they can really make the time to attend. And they are lying to themselves about their true commitment to their child's academic achievement! Tell their teacher to grade your performance. If you don't show, they send you an F. If you show up but are grumpy, you get a C minus. When you make the effort to be honestly involved, you'll get an A every time!

Every interaction with your child is ruled by *honesty trumps all*. When you don't tell your kids the truth, you can make them uncomfortable in front of their friends or other adults when your deception is revealed. Children who can count on their parent to tell the truth—even in a bad situation, even when the truth casts the parent in a bad light—knows their parent is trustworthy. You're human and you make mistakes. Be honest about them and your child will love you even more!

LOVE IS NOT A CONTRACT

Love is not a contract that demands anything—*anything*—in return.

Love is not a contract struck between you and your children. If you are a parent, your first duty is to love your children unconditionally. Unconditional love gives them an adult they can always turn to. It provides them with a security that is far more important than any fancy home or tasty food. Unconditional love nests within you for as long as you both shall live.

Love is not a contract because you love your child no matter what. You don't stop loving your son because he failed to achieve. You don't withhold love from your daughter because she misbehaved. Your love never dies in the face of drugs, crime, or values that don't match up to your own. Unconditional love is always available to them because there is no contract to break.

One of the hardest jobs for a parent is to maintain *love that is not a contract.* I want you to remember one thing: Loving your child does not mean that you must help them. At many, many points in their development, you will have to step back and allow them to fly solo. You must do this even if you know that their wings will fail and they will plummet to the ground. Love them enough to allow them to make their own mistakes, even if they keep making the same mistakes. You will always love them but you don't always have to give them money, food, or a place to live if they are on a path that leads only down.

LISTEN WITH YOUR HEART

Listening with your heart engages you with your kids every time.

Listen with your heart to hear the truth about your kids. When you tune into the wavelength of love, you pick up on subtle signals you might otherwise miss. You notice what your children say, and what they don't say. Listening with your heart creates a safe, comforting place where they can tell you everything, even the things you might not want to hear.

Listening with your heart opens entirely new pathways of communication. Instead of tromping down the same old pathway (and ending up in the same frustrating place), you'll explore a new road with your children. You'll hear how things are in their world, which has changed a lot since you were young. Listening with your heart keeps you up to date with their brave new world.

Listen with your heart by turning off your critical mind. Instead of rushing to tell your children your opinion about right and wrong, wait for them to tell their entire story. And be sure you're engaged with their words! If you catch yourself thinking about how you're going to respond or what words you want to say, you're not engaged! Be sure to catch every nuance of their tone, their expressions, and their words. Stay open and you'll hear exactly what you need to hear.

BEHAVE LIKE A PARENT

Behave like a parent even when you're tired and overwhelmed.

Behaving like a parent teaches your children to think for themselves. It provides your kids with the right amount of guidance at the right times. It keeps your family whole and functioning even in the face of extreme challenges. Behaving like a parent also means that you will forgive yourself for the times you make mistakes!

Successful parents *behave like a parent* rather than like grown-up children. You can't always have what you want. You won't always get your way. You'll be so tired you'll be very tempted to overlook your kid's bad behavior "just this once." You'll be so frustrated you'll want to shout at the first person to look at you wrong, even if that person is your child. Don't give in. Keep your emotions under control and keep it together. Behave like a parent!

Behave like a parent by making sure you have what you need! Get to know your neighbors well enough to know who you can trust in a pinch. Join a parent's social group so you can chat with adults who know where you're coming from. Connect with your child's teachers, keep the lines of communication open, and tell them (often!) how much their efforts mean to you. Every time you hear your own words, you'll feel grateful they are in your kid's life. Retreat to your bedroom for a few minutes whenever you need a break. Do things you love at least once a week as your reward! Behave like a parent by taking care of yourself.

SHARE DECISIONS

Share decisions by including your kids in different parts of the decision-making process.

Sharing decisions allows your kids to develop critical thinking skills. When they're able to participate with you in assessing a situation, they feel capable and confident in their own abilities. And because you're guiding them every step of the way, they're going to stay safe from any negative consequences that might come from making a bad decision!

Share decisions even when you don't want to. Your kids are also part of your family. They deserve a voice in what happens inside your home. If you prevent them from participating, you take away their power. You tell them that what they think and feel doesn't count. You tell them their needs aren't as important as yours, or even that their needs aren't important at all.

Share decisions in an age-appropriate way. When you're planning the family vacation, get input from teenagers on possible locations and narrow down the options provided by the entire family. As your children grow, ask their teachers to provide opportunities for them to make decisions as students. When kids are young, present them with the location and a list of things your family can do there so that everyone can pick activities together. You'll control the schedule, the length of time, and costs. Everything else can be shared!

NOURISH SPIRITUALITY

Nourish spirituality so your kids can fall back on something meaningful.

Nourish spirituality because children need it! Kids question and seek and wonder and wander. They need to know that everything in the universe is connected because that makes them want to be good people in that universe. When they realize that their lives are about more than what they want, they grow spiritually.

Nourish spirituality even if you are completely uninterested in matters of the spirit. It doesn't matter whether you've stepped away from church and don't bother with spiritual beliefs. You're older, you have set your life's path a certain way, and that's what makes you happy. Your kids, on the other hand, are just starting out! They need an internal compass to guide them when you're not there. Offer them the gift of spirituality so they can begin to make their own choices about what to believe.

Nourish spirituality by offering your own thoughts, views, beliefs, and opinions. Then step aside and allow your kids to explore other thoughts, views, beliefs, and opinions! Stand ready to help them find answers to questions that arise or explore more deeply. Recognize that a child's intensive interest doesn't mean they're definitely going down that road—it only means that things look new to them! Give them the freedom to wander around. You'll both benefit from the process.

STEP UP

Step up by getting involved in your child's school.

Stepping up at your children's school places you at ground zero for their lives and their futures. Research shows that when parents are involved with their children's education at home, the kids do better in school. When parents get involved at school, their children go farther and the schools improve.

Step up at school, because if you don't, you and your child will lose out. If you're not actively involved in the place where they spend so many hours of the day, what message does that send about learning? Even if you can't be there physically, stay involved by asking their teacher to e-mail you lesson plans, homework assignments, and daily planners. Keep them from questioning the value of an education. Yes, volunteering and tracking their lessons takes time, and it takes time away from all the other things you need to do. But how important are your children? How important is their future?

Step up at school in small increments. A lot of you won't be able to show up physically at school during the week because you're working. So make sure to volunteer for events that happen on the weekends or during the evenings. If transportation is an issue, recruit other parents with cars and make a fun outing of it for the adults. You'll send the right message to your kids—the one that says, "I care."

TEACH RESPECT

Teach respect for authority by showing respect to authority.

Every parent knows to *teach respect* for authority to their kids. But a lot of parents fail to teach respect through personal example. Your kids watch your actions much more closely than they listen to your words.

When you show respect for authority, you teach respect for authority. And that keeps them engaged in school and in life!

It's so easy to fail to *teach respect.* Parents are human beings, and we slip up. We forget that our kids are listening in on every phone call when we complain to other parents about a teacher. We don't realize that every time we frown or "tsk" at a note the principal sends home, we teach disrespect for authority. And yet we expect our kids to do as we say and not as we do! Always show respect for their teachers when you meet them. Shake their hands, listen to what they say, and thank them for the great job they're doing—in front of your child! Any issues that arise can be resolved in private. Then you and the teacher can present a unified front built on mutual respect.

Teach respect by showing respect at every moment. Remember that you don't have to like everyone or their policies. You do, however, have to respect their position. When you disagree, don't get angry or act huffy. Instead, calmly consider the issue. Then engage in an open, honest conversation with the person in charge. Not only will you model the real respect for authority you want your kids to learn, you'll frequently create a win-win situation!

RESPECT IS EARNED

Respect is earned even inside your home.

Respect is earned by everyone you work with, everyone your children meet at school, and within the walls of your home. When people respect each other, the work load gets lighter all around. Arguments happen less often and, when issues arise, even kids can control their frustration long enough to look for a solution.

Respect must be earned by teachers, administrators, classmates, and parents. You do not get a free pass just because you brought a child into the world. You, too, must earn the respect of your children. You must prove to them, day after day, that you care and that you are reliable. Do your duty for them and you will deserve their respect!

Respect is earned by being consistent in your duties as an adult. Teach your kids how to communicate so they always know how to be heard. Give your children the honesty they deserve to ensure that you don't lose their respect. Manage your anger in respectful ways.

When they disappoint you, communicate with them respectfully and you'll never lose their respect.

NEVER GIVE UP

Never give up on your kids. They're all you have.

Never give up on your children. You took responsibility for their lives the moment you decided to bring new life into the world. You are responsible for them from the day they are born to the day they leave home to forge their own lives. Use cuddling, tough love, or whatever you need to, but never give up on the people you created.

Never give up even when things are at their darkest. All kids are going to make mistakes. Some kids are going to really go off the rails and end up doing drugs, dropping out of school, or committing crimes. Never turn your back on them. Charge right into the fray by calling on the teachers for help. Find out what's happening at school and how your child responds to those events while they're on campus. You don't have to support them in a way that allows them to continue down that shadowy road but you should never give up hope that they will return to a righteous path.

A parent's toughest job can be to *never give up.* You might reach the point where you think that nothing you can do will ever make a difference. I hope that day never comes but if it does, you would be wrong. The one thing a parent can always do, the one thing that will always make a difference, is to keep loving them. It might take the rest of their lives, but you will make a difference as long as you don't give up.

TEACH LOVE

Teach love for themselves and for a spiritual power.

Teaching love is one of the greatest gifts a parent can offer a child. Having love in your life is critical to a full and fully human existence. When you teach children to love themselves, they discover confidence and security from inside. When you teach children to love a higher power, they discover the joy and safety of spirituality.

Teach love that is centered in or on education. First, teach your children to love learning. Second, teach your children to love their classmates, even the annoying ones! Third, teach them to love their teachers and the other adults at school who give so much every day. When love radiates around the educational experience, your kids will enjoy their days more and excel!

Teaching love is a tall order. It starts by loving yourself! When you show kids that you care enough to rest, to recharge, and to do things you enjoy, you demonstrate how important it is to love yourself. Teaching children how to love a higher power happens with lessons in morality, faith, and hope. No matter what beliefs you hold, share them with your kids and encourage them to explore their own beliefs. You might find that the path is full of wonderful moments!

SUPPORT THE SEARCH

Support the search your kids undertake to find themselves.

Support the search that every child will embark on toward their own true self. When you do, you can become a guide when they need it, offer comfort when they make mistakes, and help them push past the inevitable difficulties. Support the search and you'll support the best that they can become!

Supporting the search is especially important at school. When your child tells you they hate a subject, don't shut them down by telling them they have to do it anyway. Instead, ask them why they hate that topic so much. Perhaps they're really struggling with the lessons. Or perhaps they really just don't like the teacher who's presenting the lessons! They might also be suffering from bullying and don't want to go into that classroom, but they don't want to tattle on the bully by talking to a trusted adult. When you support the search by leading the search, you support their growing sense of self.

Don't be afraid to *support the search* in areas where you aren't an expert. If your kid wants to explore a career field that is outside your own experience, connect with a professional who can talk to your teen. Children who are exploring their likes and dislikes, their skills and abilities want to do new things. Give them the opportunity to try those new things and you'll support their search for themselves!

UNIVERSAL LOVE

Universal love is the understanding that people of all races and faiths deserve to be treated as fully human.

Universal love isn't some fluffy platitude that you can say and forget in the same breath. Instead, it's a way of living that welcomes the richness of the world! By teaching your kids universal love, you open them to all the wonders that the nations and cultures of our earth have to offer.

Universal love is critically important in school. When your kids head off every morning, they're going to meet other kids and adults from every walk of life. They're going to meet people whose lives and lifestyles are very similar to their own—and whose lives and lifestyles are very different. You can model universal love by being kind and caring toward their teachers. Send them to school with a flower cut from your garden. Write a thank-you note and show it to your child before you drop it in the mail. Prepare them to explore the world to its fullest by teaching them universal love!

Universal love is embodied by universal grace. Grace is the state of love that flows without need or requirement. It means that you offer love willingly and without expectation of reward and without demanding that the love be returned. When you exist in that grace, you model—and therefore teach—the universal love that will bless your children with an open and loving perspective.

LET GO

Let go of your hold on your kids to allow them the freedom to fly!

Letting go of your control over your children at the right moments develops their self-esteem. It teaches them that they can take care of themselves. Letting go allows them to make their own decisions. All of this helps them mature.

Let go of total control over school assignments as the years progress. Every new grade level brings new challenges and goals for your child. One of them should be to take another step toward independence and maturity. Talk to their teacher at the beginning of the year to discover the best goals to set. Once your children have settled into the new classroom, help them set up a routine. Run it by the teacher to make sure it works in that classroom for your child and for the teacher's methods. Then step back and allow them to run things under your supervision (not your direct control).

Let go by grounding your children with strong roots. Give them a sense that their family history is deep and long. Show them every day that their home is a safe and stable environment. Tell them (over and over and over) that no matter what, you will always love them and you will always be there for them. With you at their back and your family under their feet, they will be able to find their own way safely.

SEEDS OF SUCCESS

Plant *seeds of success* to help your children thrive throughout their lives!

Seeds of success should be planted early and often. Every part of your child's life represents change and new beginnings. By planting seeds of success all the time, you allow them to harvest multiple bounties at multiple times!

Plant *seeds of success* for education very young. Read to your kids even before they know any words themselves. Start at bedtime with fun stories. As they grow older, make reading aloud from different books a special activity for the whole family. By the time they are in middle school, you can start reading them small portions of the local news. In high school, you can read bits of national news stories to them at breakfast. You'll encourage them to explore many new things and plant the seeds of literacy and curiosity!

Seeds of success can be planted anytime. Some of your seeds will grow quickly and be harvested immediately. These are the kinds that are most appropriate for the youngest children. Other seeds need time to grow; when they are harvested, they will provide an abundance for your child. And then there are the seeds that take the longest to grow—and that never stop giving. These are the ones that are closest to your heart. They provide your children with the values that will hold them steady no matter how far into the weeds they stray!

SOFT STEPS

Soft steps reminds you to integrate step-relatives gently.

Taking a *soft-step* approach to integrating a family helps everyone at home. Your kids won't feel like they're being forced to accept a stepparent or a stepsibling. Instead, they'll have the time and the freedom to get to know the other person on their own terms. Once they do, they are much more likely to treat that person with the love due a family member.

Soft steps are critically important in your child's education. When you first introduce a stepparent, you might not want your spouse to take on any role in the child's academic efforts. The child simply might not recognize the stepparent's authority yet. Give it time to grow. Have the stepparent volunteer for a few school activities, take them along for the teacher meetings, and get them to attend extracurricular events. Then as the bond grows, the child will naturally accept the stepparent's authority over their education.

Soft steps are important at home, too. Stepparents and stepsiblings have to be introduced as equals, especially if they are relocating from their old home to the child's home. Recognize that your kids might be mourning the loss of their other parent even if they are visiting him or her on a regular basis. Help them work through the pain, and you'll set them down the path toward accepting their stepparent much more quickly. Time spent together will provide the best results!

BREAK BREAD

Break bread with your kids to preserve a specific time when you can focus on each other.

Breaking bread with your kids will deepen your relationship every day. The twenty minutes or so you spend sharing food with your child will nourish you both in meaningful ways. The calm that can set in during this time ensures that your child feels the stability you offer even when they leave the table.

Breaking bread is actually important at school, too. Twice a year, get permission from the school to visit your children and eat with them in the cafeteria. Go through the line with your kid and pick from the same foods! If the weather is nice, bring a picnic lunch and eat together outside. If there's a teacher they always talk about, invite them along! When you all chat about things that relate to schoolwork and to your lives outside of school, your child will see your teacher in a new light —as will you! You'll also meet your child's friends and see how they interact with others in a very immediate way.

Break bread together at least once every day. Mealtimes don't have to be fancy or involved; they just have to be done together. You might eat on the run or at a café. You might have time to prepare a big dinner or get up early to toast a few biscuits you bought the day before. As long as you share at least one meal with your child every day, the bond you'll form will enhance your relationship for all the hours of the day.

ALL GOOD

All good teaches kids that there is good in everything if they know how to look.

All good plants in children an idea that a spark of good resides in everyone and everything. By teaching your kids to look for that goodness, you provide them with a healthy, positive outlook on life. They become more resilient, healthier in their personalities, and even more fun loving!

All good helps your child handle the challenges of school. Every year, they walk into a new crowd and face new challenges. Throughout the year, they encounter different teachers and lessons and concepts. If your kid has a tough time doing this alone, recruit their teacher's help. Trust me, they can catch that tiny frown that means your child isn't happy! When they have the ability to find the good even in tough assignments and classmates they don't like, they are able to handle the stress much more easily.

All good provides a solid foundation for your child's development. The best way to teach a child how to locate the good in something is to mirror that yourself. When you have a tough day at work, share it with your kids and tell them about the good in that challenge. If your neighbor isn't the nicest person, tell your children one thing that is good about that person. Support your lessons with activities like taking flowers from your garden over to the not-so-nice neighbor. Your actions will resonate with your kids for years!

PACE WITH PATIENCE

Pace with patience to prevent frustration from building up.

Pace with patience to give your children the space and time they need to grow. They won't always know how to do things, and sometimes they will be just plain stubborn. When you pace yourself with patience, you allow your child the time to think things through. They receive the space in which to fail, which allows them to succeed!

Academic activities should be *paced with patience*. When homework is assigned, your children should feel as if the time they have is enough to get everything done. If they are pressured to finish up so they can perform chores, they won't do as well. Give them time to take a break before starting to ensure they come to the homework desk calm and relaxed. And set up your mornings so their journey to school is also calm and relaxed!

Pace your home life with patience to give your children the best that you have to offer. Avoid snapping at them even when something they do triggers your emotions. Recognize that they can have bad days, too, and on those days their behavior isn't going to be sterling. Offer extra comfort on their bad days to help them regain their balance. And have enough patience with your own bad days to give yourself extra comfort, too!

CHILDREN ARE PEOPLE

Children are people so accept them for who they are and not who you want them to be!

When you treat *children like people*, you recognize that they are as unique as any other human being walking the planet. You allow them to develop and expand and explore down the paths that suit them best. They will grow much more quickly than usual if they are pressured to bend in a way that just doesn't fit!

Children are people in school. Although the state and federal governments have laid down a lot of mandatory lessons, the teaching methods might not fit your child as well as the rest. Make sure the teachers know about any special challenges with reading or other skills. Recognize that not every child will have tons of friends in class, so those students might do best in a formal study group. Customize their education to maximize their learning!

Children are people in your family. They have roles as sons or daughters, as brothers or sisters. And remember that for most kids, especially when they're young, teachers can feel (and become) like a beloved relative. Just remember that your child might not fulfill those different roles in the way that child psychologists say is average. Keep an eye out for issues but recognize that most differences stem from the fact that they are unique individuals. Allow them the freedom to be who they are and they will fly!

JOIN THE JOURNEY

Join the journey your child is taking to get the most out of parenting!

Joining the journey will make the time you spend with your children much more meaningful. When you participate fully in their growth, you walk beside them during the most important moments of their lives. You're there when they need you, and you get to share the joy!

Join the journey your children take in their academic life. Participate in special events, volunteer to help with outings, and pitch in with the fundraising efforts. Every night review your children's work and talk to them about what happened in school. Be sure to ask about their friends! You'll learn more about their lives and see how their education is helping to develop their personalities.

Join the journey inside and outside the home. Attend the sports or other practice activities your children have taken up. You'll see how they are evolving. You'll also be able to see them interact with different adults and friends. These moments will become a very special part of the memories you will share all your lives.

PARENT FOR LIFE

Parent for life means once a parent, always a parent.

Parent for life is in the nature of every mother and father. No matter how old your children grow, no matter how feeble you become in your twilight years, you will always be their parent. You will always want to help, to offer advice, to comfort. Parenting is a lifelong calling that pays back for decades!

The school is a great place to prove that you are a *parent for life*. Be actively engaged with your children's education. Even during summer, you can encourage additional learning by engaging them in hobbies, taking them to museums, or downloading documentaries about things they find interesting. During the academic year, support the developmental goals your child's teacher holds by asking where your child needs to grow. Then ask how you can support those goals at home! *Parent for life* is a long-term commitment with immediate results. Because you have the ability to look far into the future and see the adult your child will become, you recognize how important your focus is on that young life. This knowledge can bolster you when you need it most—when you're tired from a long day at work, when the bickering seems endless, or when other issues just won't yield to your efforts. Know that every moment you spend tending your child today pays off long into the future!

LOVE BEING A PARENT

Love being a parent because it can be your life's greatest accomplishment.

Love being a parent because it will make you feel wonderful about your life! Taking on the role of mother or father is like heading out on a treasure hunt. Every day you find shiny gems strewn along your path. Sometimes you rub away the tarnish and discover a valuable coin. Every moment of parenting is a new discovery!

Love being the parent of school-aged children. Their journey is one of discovery, too. Along the way they unearth treasure troves of knowledge. You can help them succeed, and because what kids are learning today is so different from a generation ago, you're bound to learn new things, too! Share those moments of discovery with your kids and you'll love being a parent engaged with your child's academic efforts.

Love being a parent by paying attention to the little things. And don't forget the guilty pleasures! Sneak a cookie with your kid once in a while. Stay out late with them—past their bedtime, not past yours! Catch their excitement over things that seem common and boring to you. You might find that what's old is new again!

BANISH BLAME

Banish blame because parents can't control everything.

Banish blame that doesn't belong to you. Yes, parents are responsible for their children, but if you've done everything you can possibly do and your kids still don't turn out well, don't punish yourself. Your children are their own people. Sometimes your best effort just won't reach them. *Banish blame* when it comes to your child's education. Some kids aren't suited for certain subjects no matter what government mandates say. Other kids aren't going to motivate themselves to step up and get a passing grade in every class. Do what you can to support their education by introducing them to alternative forms of learning. And leave blame at the door!

Banish blame in other areas where your child doesn't meet expectations. If your teenagers just won't go get a job, make sure they're doing something around the house to earn their keep. When your preteens constantly break the rules, do what you can to keep them safe. If your youngest kids refuse to do their chores no matter what the consequences, keep trying, but banish blame from your mind and your heart!

KEEP THE FUTURE

If one of your children dies, *keep the future* for your other children.

Keep the future for your surviving children in the event that one child dies. Your grief—and theirs—needs to run its course in a way that is appropriate and respectful of the lives that are continuing.

Keep the future for all your children by supporting them as they return to school after the loss of a sibling. Some kids might be too young to fully understand the loss. Others might be too immature to handle their grief. Assess each child's personality to determine the right time to return to school. And when they do return, be sure their teacher knows where they stand emotionally. Ask if they can be given extra support or a few breaks in a quiet space. Their teachers are there to help!

Keep the future alive by comforting your children—and allowing them to comfort you. Know that although your pain is intense, you still have other children who will shine brightly all their lives. Support them as best you can. If you need help, call in a relative or a trusted friend to pick up the slack. Do not allow your other children to suffer more than they need to during this period.

VOW OF NONVIOLENCE

Take a *vow of nonviolence* to lead your family down a happy, healthy, supportive path.

A *vow of nonviolence* should be part of every family. When parents refuse to beat or verbally berate their children, they're promising to raise them in a wholesome way. When children take the nonviolent vow, their relationships with their siblings grow stronger. They're able to diffuse tense situations with more mature methods. And that helps them outside the home, too!

The *vow of nonviolence* applies to time spent on school property. Every child will likely have to deal with a bully at some point. Even if the other child doesn't threaten them physically, they might harass your child so much that your son or daughter wants to strike out. Show them early on how to deal with these situations emotionally. And give them plenty of options for getting help from teachers and counselors!

A happy home integrates a *vow of nonviolence* into its fabric. Parents never beat their children. Siblings are not allowed to hit, kick, bite, pinch, or pull hair. And no one is allowed to use violent words. Calling someone stupid, ignorant, lazy, or any mean word is just as harmful from the mouth of a relative as from the mouth of a bully. Love conquers every issue. Let your words ring with love!

THE SUPREME GIFT

Children are *the supreme gift* for any parent.

Knowing that your children are a *supreme gift* reminds you to cherish them every day. Every little milestone that they achieve (and there will be many) creates another wonderful memory for the lucky parent who pays attention.

Give your *supreme gift* the limitless gift of an education. Make sure that their every step in school is supported by individuals who recognize how special they are. Get to know the teachers who spend so much time with your child. Visit the principal and other administrators once a year. When you make the personal connection, you'll ensure that you are able to help your children get the best out of their academic experience!

Treat your *supreme gift* with the special care they deserve. Every night, be sure to hug them or hold their hand. Physical touch is incredibly important to all human beings, and especially to kids. A gentle, loving touch speaks volumes! Tell your child every morning and evening that you love them and that you will always love them. Your affection and care should never be in doubt.

FLEX FAST

Flex fast to adjust your methods on the fly.

Flex fast is all about taking things as they come. With kids around, the one thing you can be sure of is that issues will crop up! Being able to shift your approach—and sometimes even what you're doing—lets you cope with everything the moment it changes. And that reduces your stress and makes your life easier!

Flex fast around school issues. Your children are going to forget to bring home information about some event until the day before. Your children might join a team or extracurricular activity and then change their mind about participating. Every time, you have to remain flexible enough to help them through the situation. Keep their teachers updated on any changes and the reasons why you have allowed those changes. You'll give your children the confidence to follow their hearts, and you'll be able to emphasize the importance of paying attention to schedules!

Flex fast around issues that crop up in the home. Your children might be going along very well until they start a new grade level or summer arrives. Suddenly their world falls apart! You need to find out why your child is depressed or upset or angry—and fast. When you're used to flexing fast, you know immediately what can be pushed aside and what can be cancelled altogether. Then your children get the attention they need so that the issue can be resolved.

KNOW YOUR LIMITS

Know your limits because every parent has them, and every parent hits them.

Knowing your limits helps you keep calm and patient in adverse situations. It ensures that your quality time together with your child is really top-notch! By knowing when to say no and when to turn aside from the limit you're approaching, you're able to stay balanced within yourself. And that keeps your relationship with your child in balance.

Know your limits around school-related activities. You won't be able to volunteer for every special event. You might not be able to attend every one of your children's performances if they're involved with a lot of after-school activities. Let your children know that not taking on too much is a way to take care of yourself, and you'll set a great example for their lives as adults!

Know your limits as a parent. If you feel your emotions start to spin out of control, put yourself into a time-out! When the burden of everything you need to get done in a day feels overwhelming, take five minutes to walk around outside or just gaze up at the clouds. A break of even a few minutes does wonders to refresh your mind and help you engage on a new level!

PARENTS MATTER

Never doubt that *parents matter.*

Parents matter every minute of the day. Even when you doubt your ability or your approach, what you do matters in the life of your child. Even when you make mistakes, your presence gives your child stability. Even when you feel overwhelmed, your efforts build a stable foundation for your kids.

Parents matter to a child's education. Remember that your attitude toward schooling is one of the biggest drivers of your child's efforts. When you stay positive about school and impress the need for an education on your kids, they are much more likely to strive and excel in the academic realm. So support their teachers in direct and meaningful ways. Always praise the teachers when you talk about them with your children. And remember that it's nice if you send a note to the teacher to let them know how great they are!

Parents matter in the smallest and largest ways. Your involvement in the life of your children sets the stage for how they will feel about themselves for the rest of their lives! When you shuffle your priorities so that your kids come out on top, they recognize that they are valuable and that they are loved. When you know that you matter, you automatically become the role model they need!

ADAPT AND EVOLVE

Adapt and evolve with your children to keep pace with their growth.

Adapt and evolve your methods and approach to ensure that you are always taking the best steps for your child. You'll start with a certain set of rules or habits. As your child grows, their personality will expand in ways that make certain rules and habits less effective. When you adapt and evolve, you keep pace with your child!

Adapt and evolve your approach to your child's education. Ensure that they feel safe on the trip to school by escorting them or teaming them up with a buddy their age. If they get the chance to enroll in advanced classes, raise your support to the higher level they need for that course.

Parents must *adapt and evolve* all the time. Make sure you're staying in step by reassessing your own activities and habits whenever your child hits an important milestone. At the start of a new school year, ask yourself whether you can provide them with more responsibility in certain areas. Whenever school lets out for the long break, study the plan for that break to see whether you can interact with your children differently from the way you did the previous year. Keep adapting and evolving, and you'll keep your status as a premium parent!

NEED OR WANT?

When you decide whether an action or thing is a *need or a want*, you're able to clear the clutter from your to-do list.

Parsing things into categories called *need or want* helps you determine which ones should be done. It also helps you prioritize activities when several things need to be done. And by clearing off the wants, many of which are illusory ideas of perfection, you become far more effective!

Need or want can help your children focus on their academic success. They might want to make every line perfect in a report or story they're getting ready to turn in. But if that means they don't have time for any of their other homework, then you'll have to help them decide when the need has been met. Tune into what their teacher has to say about this. They have the experience to judge your child's abilities, so they are a great resource. You'll help your kids reach all their academic goals!

Need or want helps you become more effective. Frequently, parents feel overwhelmed by all the things on their lists. Every time you know that you're overbooked, take a good look at that list. What is an absolute need? Among the needed tasks, do they have to be completed fully or can you do just enough laundry to get through the next few days? Determine the actual needs and you'll have more time for the happy wants!

Final Words

Always a Parent

Always a parent means that in good times and in bad, you offer your children the fullness of your love.

Always a parent is the shining glory that arrives at the moment of birth and stays with you for the rest of your life. In the depths of terrible crises, you will always be a parent who cares. At the height of your child's triumphs, you will always be a parent who is proud. Even when your older children leave to start their own lives, you will always provide them with a home in your heart!

In a *Psychology Today* blog post, therapist Mark Sichel talked about *always being a parent.* He shared that when he was young, his parents cut off contact. Nevertheless, he knew that a parent remains a parent no matter how bad things get. While addressing issues can be difficult, once those issues have been resolved, the family should take steps to make things right between them. Their relationships will grow stronger!

If you're reading this book, I'm sure you are *always a parent* to your child. But sometimes we do things that aren't very loving. If ever you find yourself yelling, stop. Only talk to your kids when you can be calm and find a way to connect. At the same time, don't hover! Be a parent who guides kids through their own decisions so they can grow. And if ever you feel overwhelmed, focus on your heart. I guarantee that you will discover deep reserves of love!

Sichel, Mark. "Once a Parent, Always a Parent: One Mother's Resignation by Literary Defamation." *Psychology Today* blog. Retrieved from https://www.psychologytoday.com/blog/the-therapist-is-in/200903/once-parent-always-parent-one-mother-s-resignation-literary.

About the Author

For forty-three years, **Dr. Barbara D. Culp** has dedicated herself to education. After teaching at the elementary and middle school levels, she became the principal of a large elementary school and was selected as Principal of the Year. Currently, she is a part-time clinical supervisor for Brenau University's School of Education; she recently founded a tutorial service for public, private, charter, and parochial schools. Dr. Culp graduated from Morris Brown College and Atlanta University with a master's degree and an education doctorate degree in administration and supervision. She has conducted workshops and training programs on classroom management and differentiated instruction.

CPSIA information can be obtained
at www.ICGtesting.com
Printed in the USA
BVOW08s0024011216
469368BV00001B/1/P